DECEMBER 2024

SUN	MON	TUE	WED	THU	FRI	SAT
1	2	3	4	5	6	7
8	9	10	11	12	13	14
15	16	17	18	19	20	21
22	23	24	25	26	27	28
29	30	31				

Dear Child Care Professional,

Thanks for choosing the *2025 Redleaf Calendar-Keeper*!

As in years past, this edition of the *Redleaf Calendar-Keeper* contains all the trusted worksheets, expense charts, and tools you rely on to maintain accurate and detailed business records throughout the year. The more information you capture in your *Redleaf Calendar-Keeper*, the more money and time you will save on your taxes.

In addition to all of the record-keeping benefits, a number of great features and items of note are included in this year's *Redleaf Calendar-Keeper*.

Antiracist Themes, Children's Books, and Activities for Young Children
The more opportunities children have to see and share experiences with people of diverse races (including through books like *All the Colors We Are* and *The Colors of Us*), the less preference they show toward their own race. Along with recommended children's books, throughout the *2025 Redleaf Calendar-Keeper* you will find antiracist activities for children you can easily incorporate into your day. It is never too early to start teaching the value of diversity.

Up-to-Date USDA Reimbursement Guidelines
Every year we research for updates to the United States Department of Agriculture's (USDA's) Child and Adult Care Food Program (CACFP) and integrate any new information so you won't have to worry about identifying the new regulations yourself. Still unsure of ounce equivalents? Go to the Calendar-Keeper web page or RedleafPress.org for easy-to-understand charts.

Literacy Corner
Literacy development starts early in life and is important in developing cognitive skills. The educational and emotional benefits of reading together prepare young children to succeed in school. Each month you will find two suggested children's books that correspond with the month's theme. Many of the 24 children's books, including *All the Colors We Are/Todos los colores de nuestra piel* by Katie Kissinger and *Bree Finds a Friend* by Mike Huber, are available at RedleafPress.org/Childrens-Books.

Activities for Children
Ninety percent of brain development occurs by the time a child is five years old. That means those early years are really important! All the inspiration and activities featured in this year's Calendar-Keeper are from Redleaf Press books, including *I Like Myself: Fostering Positive Racial Identity in Young Black Children* by Toni Sturdivant, PhD, and *Teaching STEM in the Early Years: Activities for Integrating Science, Technology, Engineering, and Mathematics*, 2nd Edition, by Sally Moomaw, EdD. Use these ideas to promote healthy brain development and social-emotional learning in the children you care for.

The Experienced Provider
As a child care provider, you have to address many challenges throughout the day. This year's Calendar-Keeper has advice from a variety of Redleaf Press resources, including *Loose Parts in Action: The Essential How-To Guide* by Lisa Daly, *The Many Stories of Our Beloved Community: Honoring Young Children's Kinship and Connections with the World* by Rukia Monique Rogers, and *Protecting Your Family Child Care Business: Preventing and Addressing Regulatory Challenges* by Sharon Woodward.

Have a wonderful year!

Your friends at Redleaf Press

The Think Small Institute

In our third year, the Think Small Institute offers best-in-class, nationally recognized eLearning content using Reflective Practice, Anti-Racist Pedagogy, and Trauma-Informed Care to specifically meet your needs. Our Family Child Care subject matter experts embed best practices in all of our content and include home-based environments. Additionally, our family child care subject matter experts include Nikki Darling-Kuria, Director of Think Small Institute and Redleaf Press, and Dr. Ellaine B. Miller, Board President of the National Association for Family Child Care.

Are you interested in becoming a subject matter expert and contributing to the development of eLearning content? Please contact us at institute@thinksmall.org.

Thinksmall.org/shop

Redleaf Press Family Child Care Resources

The Business of Family Child Care: Contracts and Policies
Most family child care providers would rather care for children than write and enforce contracts and policies, but taking care of the children is only part of the job. Contracts and policies are another important part of running a business. This video can help you understand how to establish a good business relationship with the families you serve by creating clear contracts and policies and enforcing them fairly.

#548029-CK25 $49.95

The Business of Family Child Care: Record-Keeping
Most family child care providers would rather care for children than spend time keeping records. But record keeping is an important part of running a business. This training video can help you understand proper record-keeping strategies, help lower taxes, and save family child care providers money.

#547329-CK25 $79.95

The Redleaf Complete Forms Kit
For Both Family Child Care and Center-Based Programs, Revised Edition

Keep your business organized and save hours of time! This CD-ROM includes more than 150 child care forms—the most comprehensive and professionally presented forms available. CD-ROM.

#546520-CK25 $24.95

Infant Daily Report or Toddler Daily Report
Parents fill out the top half of these handy sheets at drop-off, and you report diapering, feeding, napping, and eating information on the bottom half. You'll receive three tablets, each with 60 pages—a six-month supply.

#112101-CK25 $14.95   #112701-CK25 $12.95

Daily Lesson Planner
Schedule your day with this planning aid. It has space to conveniently keep track of activities, learning centers, and more. The planner is on a six-day-per-week cycle. You'll receive three tablets, which are three-hole punched, each with 60 pages—a six-month supply.

#112501-CK25 $14.95

Injury Log
Document injuries on these weekly sheets. Each form is organized with areas to record all relevant information. The tablet is three-hole punched and has 55 forms.

#112301-CK25 $9.95

The Redleaf Family Child Care Curriculum Complete Set
Sharon Woodward

Save almost $20 when you buy the set!

#541080-CK25 $59.95

This starter set includes:

The Redleaf Family Child Care Curriculum, 2nd Edition
Provide high-quality care with this easy-to-use complete curriculum designed for family child care programs with mixed-age children. 256 pgs.

#544144-CK25 $44.95

The Redleaf Family Child Care Curriculum Developmental Assessment, Revised Edition (10 copies)
Observe and record a child's growth and development with the *Developmental Assessment*.

#544168-CK25 $16.95

The Redleaf Family Child Care Curriculum Family Companion, Revised Edition (10 Copies)
Give families an overview of the *Family Child Care Curriculum*.

#544779-CK25 $10.95

The Redleaf Family Child Care Curriculum Developmental Assessment Guide, Revised Edition
This guide walks you through the process of using the *Developmental Assessment* tool and provides tips to help you communicate with families.

#544786-CK25 $6.95

> *The Redleaf Family Child Care Curriculum* and supplemental materials are available in Spanish! Visit RedleafPress.org for more information (#547177-CK25)

Family Child Care Homes
Creative Spaces for Children to Learn
Linda J. Armstrong

Create warm and inviting places where children feel at home. Loaded with photographs of inventive and practical spaces, you will find inspiration to create your own stimulating and cozy environment. Softbound, 216 pgs.

#540757-CK25 $49.95

Protecting Your Family Child Care Business
Preventing and Addressing Regulatory Challenges
Sharon Woodward

Protect your family child care business—your livelihood and the heart of your home from citations, allegations, and infractions. Softbound, 144 pgs.

#548371-CK25 $21.95

Save Time and Money Using the *Redleaf Calendar-Keeper*

For 48 years, the *Redleaf Calendar-Keeper* has saved countless hours of record keeping for family child care providers across the country. It has also helped hundreds of thousands of providers to significantly reduce their taxes.

2025

The *Redleaf Calendar-Keeper* is part of a series of record-keeping resources from Redleaf Press that includes the following titles:

- *Family Child Care Record-Keeping Guide,* **9th edition**: Identifies over 1,000 business deductions
- *Family Child Care Tax Workbook and Organizer*: Use it to do your own taxes
- *Family Child Care Tax Companion*: Use it to educate your tax professional

With these resources, you can keep accurate and detailed records that may mean big tax savings. Here are some important tips for using the *Redleaf Calendar-Keeper* most efficiently.

Three Key Record-Keeping Rules

1. Save receipts for all expenses associated with cleaning, repairing, and maintaining your home.
2. Record all meals served to the children in your care on a daily basis, including all meals not reimbursed by the Food Program.
3. For at least two months, carefully track all the hours you use your home for business, particularly the hours you spend cleaning, preparing activities, and doing other business-related tasks when the children are not present.

How the *Redleaf Calendar-Keeper* Makes Filing Taxes Easier

Virtually all providers must file IRS Form 1040 Schedule C. It is easier to complete the Schedule C when you keep track of your expenses on the *Redleaf Calendar-Keeper*, which uses the same categories that appear on the Schedule C. In fact, the expenses on the monthly expense report pages are listed in the exact order that they appear on the Schedule C. In addition, we have included five expense categories at the end of the second monthly expense report page: food, toys, household items, cleaning supplies, and activity expenses. These expense categories do not appear directly on the Schedule C, but we've created them to make it easier for you to enter your expenses on the Schedule C. We recommend that you use the series of blank lines under "Other Expenses" on the back of the Schedule C as a place to record these expense categories or other expense categories you have created.

It is important to understand that business expenses can be recorded under any category. For example, children's birthday cards can be recorded under supplies or activity expenses. You can cross out some categories listed in the *Redleaf Calendar-Keeper* and customize the categories for your own use. We left space on these pages to rename a category or to add more categories. In the end, all of your expenses will be totaled on the Schedule C, so you do not need to worry about the placement of an expense in a particular category.

To make it easier to enter expenses under the categories on the *Redleaf Calendar-Keeper* and the Schedule C, we have identified more than 1,000 allowable deductions and their expense categories in the *Family Child Care Record-Keeping Guide*, 9th edition, by Tom Copeland, available from Redleaf Press.

How to Track 100% Business Expenses

It is important that you identify which items are used 100% for business because they are worth more in deductions than items partially used for business. Individual items used 100% for business should be identified as such on the receipt. There are several ways items can be entered in the *Redleaf Calendar-Keeper*. You can write "100%" next to the expense when entering it on the monthly expense report. The 100% items should be added up separately at the end of the year. A Time-Space percentage should be used on all other items in each expense category. For example, let's say you have six items of supplies used 100% for business, totaling $200. Another 25 supply items are used both for business and for your family, totaling $1,000. If your Time-Space percentage is 40%, you can deduct $400 of the shared supplies ($1,000 x 40%) plus the $200 for the 100% business supplies, for a total supplies expense of $600.

Another way to track this on the *Redleaf Calendar-Keeper* is to create two expense categories for supplies. The supplies category already printed on the *Redleaf Calendar-Keeper* could be labeled "100% Supplies." The blank column next to it could be labeled "Shared Supplies." Supplies purchased throughout the year could be listed under the appropriate category. You should claim 100% of the supplies in the first category and the Time-Space percentage of the supplies in the second category. You can eliminate or combine the infrequently used expense categories shown on the calendar in order to have enough space to create the two expense categories that you need for your more frequent expenses.

How to Track Expenses When a Receipt Includes More Than One Expense Category

You can list all of the expenses from one receipt in one category, rather than splitting the receipt between two or more categories. For example, if a receipt has three toy items and two office-expense items, all of the expenses could be listed under either category. Simply decide which category to enter the total expense in and enter it once under that category. A more time-consuming option is to enter the date, check number, store name, and purchase amount for the office expenses on the first monthly expense report page, and the same information again, along with the purchase amount for the toys, on the second monthly expense report page. Either option will work, but remember, it is all added together in the end!

Child and Adult Care Food Program

Money received from the Food Program for children other than your own should be reported as income on your tax form. Money you receive for your own children, if you are income-eligible, is not taxable. Income from the Food Program can be recorded on either the attendance and payment log or the payment and income record. On the attendance and payment log, you can keep a monthly and year-to-date total of Food Program income, parent fees, and other income and still arrive at a year-to-date total income amount. This can help you track your income by category each year.

	FOOD PROGRAM INCOME RECVD	PARENT FEE INCOME RECVD	OTHER INCOME RECVD
FEBRUARY INCOME	$720	$1,500	—
BALANCE FORWARD	$710	$1,400	—
TOTAL Y-T-D INCOME	$1,430	$2,900	—

Using the *Redleaf Calendar-Keeper* with the Standard Meal Allowance Rule

You have two choices for claiming your food expenses. You can keep track of all business and personal food expenses and enter these amounts in the food column on the monthly expense report. Or you can use the standard meal allowance rule, which does not require you to track any food expenses or save any food receipts. For details about claiming food expenses, see the *Family Child Care Record-Keeping Guide*, 9th edition.

To use the standard meal allowance rule, you must maintain records that include the name of each child; the dates and hours of their attendance in care; and the number of breakfasts, lunches, dinners, and snacks served. How you can best use the *Redleaf Calendar-Keeper* to keep these records depends on whether you participate in the Food Program.

IF YOU ARE ON THE FOOD PROGRAM

Your monthly claim form contains all the information you need to track the reimbursed meals you served. Serving sizes for recipes in the *Redleaf Calendar-Keeper* are for ages three to five; adjust your serving according to the children in your care. Save these forms and put the totals on the year-end meal tally on page 95. You can also record the nonreimbursed meals and snacks you served on your monthly claim forms, or you can use the *Redleaf Calendar-Keeper* in one of two ways:

- Track nonreimbursed meals using the meal form on page 94. Photocopy this page, and use one form for each week of the year. You can also download this form at www.redleafpress.org (on the *Redleaf Calendar-Keeper* product page).
- Track nonreimbursed meals using the monthly attendance and payment log. On a separate line for each child, enter the number of nonreimbursed meals served, and total them at the bottom of the form each month.

IF YOU ARE NOT ON THE FOOD PROGRAM

Make sure you fill out the attendance and payment log each month with each child's name and his or her days and hours of attendance.

To track your meals and snacks, use the *Redleaf Calendar-Keeper* in one of two ways:

- Track all your meals and snacks using the meal form on page 94. Photocopy this page, and use one form for each week of the year. You can also download this form at www.redleafpress.org (on the *Redleaf Calendar-Keeper* product page).
- Track all your meals and snacks using the monthly attendance and payment log. On a separate line for each child, enter the number of meals and snacks served, and total them at the bottom of the form each month.

However you track your food expenses, enter the number of reimbursed and nonreimbursed meals on the year-end meal tally on page 95. Fill in the rest of the chart to calculate your food deduction.

How to Use the *Redleaf Calendar-Keeper* to Track Your Hours

There is a place at the top of each month's calendar to record and total the number of hours you care for children and the number of hours you work each month on business-related activities (such as cleaning, planning lessons, preparing meals, keeping records, and so on) when children are not present. A space to fill in your year-to-date total is also provided.

Carefully keeping track of the hours you work in your home will make the biggest difference in reducing your taxes. This is because your work hours are used in a Time-Space calculation that will determine how much of your house expenses you can deduct. These house expenses include your property tax, mortgage interest, utilities, homeowners insurance, house depreciation, house repairs, home improvements, and personal-property depreciation.

HOURS CHILDREN ARE IN YOUR HOME

Record all of the hours children are in your home on the attendance and payment log. You can also track irregular hours in the daily calendar squares. For example:

Leah's normal hours are 7 AM to 5 PM. Total extra hours this week: 16 hours, 45 minutes

SUN	MON	TUE	WED	THU	FRI	SAT
	Lyssa leaves 5:30 PM, 30 min.		William arrives 6:45 AM, 15 min.		Hanielle stays overnight, arrives 5 PM	Parents pick up Harielle 9 AM, 16 hrs.

CLEANING, COOKING, AND PREPARING ACTIVITIES

The hours you spend preparing for your business when children are not present can be counted in the calculation of the Time-Space percentage. You may record these business hours in one of two ways. The first method is to mark your *Redleaf Calendar-Keeper* each time you are engaged in business activities. The IRS may challenge you by arguing that some of the hours reported were spent in personal activities. To avoid this, record personal activities separately. For example:

SUN	MON	TUE	WED	THU	FRI	SAT
4 PM, business cleaning, 1 hr. 5 PM, personal cleaning, 1 hr. 8 PM, business cooking, 1 hr.	7 PM, business cleaning, 1 hr.		7 AM, business cleaning, 1 hr. 7 PM, personal cleaning, 1 hr.	7 PM, business cooking, 30 min.	7 PM, business cleaning, 1 hr.	8:30 AM, plan trip to park, 30 min.

The second method is to prepare in advance a weekly or monthly schedule that indicates when you plan to spend time on business activities. Such a schedule is likely to be accepted by the IRS if it is kept regularly and followed carefully. You may use the *Redleaf Calendar-Keeper* to prepare your schedule, or you may write it out in a separate notebook. For example:

SUN	MON	TUE	WED	THU	FRI	SAT
1 PM, business cleaning, 1 hr. 2 PM, personal cleaning, 1 hr.	6 AM, business cleaning, 1 hr. 7 PM, personal cleaning, 1 hr.		7 PM, personal cleaning, 1 hr. 8 PM, business cooking, 1 hr.		7 PM, personal cleaning, 1 hr.	

Note: You can detail your plans for one week in the month and let it represent what you will do every week in the month.

PARENT INTERVIEWS AND PHONE CALLS

Record the amount of time you spend outside of regular business hours interviewing parents or talking to parents on the phone.

RECORD KEEPING

Record the time you spend record keeping, planning menus, preparing shopping lists, balancing your checkbook, or doing financial bookkeeping for your business. For example:

SUN	MON	TUE	WED	THU	FRI	SAT
1 — 8 AM, balance checkbook, 30 min.	2	3 — 7 AM, talk to Hugo's mother, 15 min.	4	5	6 — 5 PM, interview the Bzdoks, 1 hr.	7 — 9 PM, plan menus, 1 hr.
8 — 10 PM, call from Sia's father, Sia is ill, 20 min.	9	10	11	12	13	14 — 9 PM, plan menus, 1 hr.

Notes on Record Keeping
- Review the record-keeping notes on your *Redleaf Calendar-Keeper* at the end of each month to make sure you recorded all your business activities.
- You may not count hours spent away from your home in your Time-Space percentage. This includes time spent shopping or transporting children to school.
- Do not count hours spent on business activities while children are in your care.

For a complete explanation of the Time-Space percentage, refer to chapter 3 of the *Family Child Care Record-Keeping Guide*, 9th edition. (For information about the *Family Child Care Record-Keeping Guide*, 9th edition, see page 66 of the *Redleaf Calendar-Keeper*.)

Attendance and Payment Log

Here are some examples of ways to use the attendance and payment log. Remember, the system to use is the one that works best for you.

EXAMPLE A

Provider has steady attendance, both full-time and part-time child care, but no drop-ins. She is paid whether the child is there or not.

Method 1: Provider enters drop-off and pickup times and records total hours in attendance. Payments are recorded on the payment and income record or on the attendance and payment log. This is the preferred method if you are using the IRS standard meal allowance rate because it shows when children are present.

Method 2: Provider checks (✔) attendance and records total hours in attendance. Parent payments are recorded in the same way as Method 1.

Method 3: Provider writes in total hours in attendance every day and records weekly payment in the TOTAL column of the attendance and payment log.

JANUARY ATTENDANCE AND PAYMENT LOG

CHILD'S NAME	S	M	T	W	T	F	S	TOTAL
Kenady		7/5	7/5	7/5	7/5	7/5		50hrs / $300

CHILD'S NAME	S	M	T	W	T	F	S	TOTAL
Kenady		✔	✔	✔	✔	✔		50hrs / $300

CHILD'S NAME	S	M	T	W	T	F	S	TOTAL
Kenady		10	10	10	10	10		50hrs / $300

EXAMPLE B

Provider does only part-time child care. She is paid by the hour.

Method 1: Provider enters drop-off and pickup times and records total hours in attendance. Payments are recorded on the payment and income record or on the attendance and payment log.

Method 2: Provider uses two lines, noting drop-off and pickup times on the first line, totaling the number of hours in attendance each day on the second line, and recording the total hours in attendance each week in the Saturday column. Payments are recorded in the TOTAL column of the attendance and payment log or on the payment and income record.

CHILD'S NAME	S	M	T	W	T	F	S	TOTAL HRS
Leah			3/5		3/6			5
Theo		8/10		8/10				4

CHILD'S NAME	S	M	T	W	T	F	S	TOTAL
Leah			3/5		3/6			
			2		3		5	$30
Theo		8/10		8/10				
		2		2			4	$24

PAYMENT AND INCOME RECORD FOR JANUARY

CHILD'S NAME	JANUARY					JAN TOTAL
	2	8	15	22	29	
Leah	$30					
Theo	$24					

EXAMPLE C

Provider has a steady full-time child (Kenady), a steady part-time child (Theo), and a drop-in child (Ali). She uses a combination of methods—Example A, Method 3 (Kenady) and Example B, Method 1 (Theo and Ali).

CHILD'S NAME	S	M	T	W	T	F	S	TOTAL HRS
Kenady		10	10	10	10	10		50
Theo		8/10		8/10		8/10		6
Ali				1/4				3

House Expenses Worksheet—see page 84

This chart is designed for recording your utilities and other home expenses. Space is provided for you to record the portion of these expenses that can be claimed as business expenses on your federal income tax return.

Income Tax Worksheet—see page 85

After totaling your expenses for December, enter the yearly amounts on the income tax worksheet. From here you can easily transfer your expenses to the Schedule C.

Payment and Income Record—see pages 86–93

These eight pages for recording your income are an alternative to the attendance and payment log. You can use the attendance and payment log to record attendance only and use the payment and income record to record income. To use these pages, write in the date you expect parents to pay you. In the correct space, record the amount (and the check number) and then the total for the month. At the bottom of the page, include Food Program income and any other income you receive. For the second, third, and fourth quarters, a space is provided for the balance carried forward. A paper clip or piece of tape on the edge of the current payment and income record page will make it easy to find in the *Redleaf Calendar-Keeper*.

PAYMENT AND INCOME RECORD FOR JANUARY

CHILD'S NAME	JANUARY					JAN TOTAL
	2	8	15	22	29	
Leah	4130 $62.00	4229 59.00	4275 89.00	4301 75.00	4362 68.00	353.00
Theo	Cash 50.00	Cash 50.00	Cash 50.00	Cash 50.00	Cash 50.00	250.00

Emergency Phone Numbers—see pages 96 and 97

Although you should have additional information for each child, this form provides quick access to the basic information. You may want to make a photocopy of this sheet to take with you on outings or field trips. There are lines for your own address and phone number because this information may be needed in an emergency, and you may not be the person making the emergency phone call.

Emergency Drill Record—see page 98

The emergency drill record will help you stay organized and keep an accurate record of this important routine. There is space to record a fire drill and one other emergency drill (for example, storm, tornado, or earthquake) for each month. Faithful practice and good records help keep everyone safe.

Published by Redleaf Press
10 Yorkton Court
St. Paul, MN 55117
www.redleafpress.org

© 2025 by Redleaf Press

All rights reserved. Unless otherwise noted on a specific page, no portion of this publication may be reproduced or transmitted in any form or by any means, electronic or mechanical, including photocopying, recording, or capturing on any information storage and retrieval system, without permission in writing from the publisher, except by a reviewer, who may quote brief passages in a critical article or review to be printed in a magazine or newspaper, or electronically transmitted on radio, television, or the internet.

Forty-eighth edition 2025
Senior editor: Melissa York
Cover design: Renee Hammes
Cover image © Adobe Stock
Printed in the United States of America
ISBN 978-1-60554-841-8

Redleaf Press is the publishing division of Think Small.

Please note: Because dates for certain holidays change from year to year, we cannot guarantee their accuracy. Check with your local library if you have questions. The observance of all Jewish and Islamic holidays begins at sundown the previous day.

www.redleafpress.org
800-423-8309

JANUARY 2025

Hours Worked	
Previous Total	
No. Hours Open*	
Other Hours Worked**	
Year-to-Date Total	

* "No. Hours Open" refers to hours from when the first child arrived to when the last child left (not your advertised work hours).
** "Other Hours Worked" refers to hours spent on business activities in the home (cleaning, meal preparation, activity planning, and so on) when children are not present.

SUN	MON	TUE	WED	THU	FRI	SAT
DECEMBER 2024 / FEBRUARY 2025			**1** New Year's Day	**2**	**3**	**4**
5	**6** Fire Drill Day / Record your vehicle's odometer reading	**7**	**8** Severe Storm Drill Day	**9**	**10**	**11**
12	**13**	**14**	**15** 2024 4th quarter estimated taxes due	**16**	**17**	**18**
19	**20** Martin Luther King Jr. Day	**21**	**22**	**23**	**24**	**25**
26	**27**	**28**	**29** Chinese New Year	**30**	**31** Call your local R & R agency; update your service	

Are you ready for tax season? Order your 2024 tax products now!

JANUARY

Celebrating Cultures

We share songs and tales and food,
Making new friends feels so good!

Recipes

Noodles with Peanut Butter Sauce

3 ounces uncooked whole grain spaghetti noodles
11 ounces uncooked boneless skinless chicken breast
3 cups chopped frozen broccoli
3 tablespoons smooth peanut butter
3 tablespoons soy sauce
1 tablespoon cider vinegar
1 tablespoon sugar
½ teaspoon fresh ginger, grated
1 clove garlic, minced
1 teaspoon cornstarch
Cilantro, chopped green onion, and lime wedges for serving (optional)

1. Boil 1 cup water. Break noodles in half and add to boiling water. Cook, stirring occasionally, until al dente, about 8 minutes. Drain.
2. Coat a skillet with nonstick cooking spray. Brown chicken on all sides on medium-high heat for 8–10 minutes. Add broccoli and cook for 10 more minutes. Chicken should reach an internal temperature of 165° F.
3. In a small microwavable bowl, combine 2 tablespoons warm water with peanut butter, soy sauce, cider vinegar, sugar, ginger, and garlic. Microwave sauce for 30 seconds, whisk, and microwave for 30 more seconds. Sauce will look stringy.
4. In a small bowl, combine 1 tablespoon warm water with the cornstarch to make a slurry. Whisk into peanut butter sauce and microwave 30 seconds until thick, then whisk again.
5. In a large bowl, toss together the chicken, broccoli, noodles, and sauce. Serve with cilantro, green onions, and lime wedges if desired.

Yield: 6 servings, ¾ cup each
Meal Component: Meat/Meat Alternate, Grain, Vegetable

Serving sizes are for ages 3–5. Guidelines for the proper credit of food may vary in some states. Please check with the CACFP in your state for more information.

Menu of the Month

Breakfast
Milk
Whole Grain Cereal
Bananas

Morning Snack
Water
Hard-Boiled Egg Halves
Red Pepper Slices

Lunch
Milk
Noodles with Peanut Butter Sauce* (WG)
Mandarin Oranges

Afternoon Snack
Water
Curried Chicken Wraps* (WG)

*Indicates recipes of the month.
(WG) Indicates whole grain
Recipes adapted from the Institute of Childhood Nutrition.

Curried Chicken Wraps

¼ cup nonfat plain Greek yogurt
¼ teaspoon curry powder
¼ cup diced cooked skinless chicken breast
1 cup diced fresh apples (unpeeled)
6 tablespoons golden raisins
3 whole wheat tortillas, at least 1½ ounces each

1. In a medium bowl, combine yogurt and curry powder. Using a rubber spatula, fold in chicken, apples, and raisins.
2. Place ½ cup chicken salad in the center of each tortilla. Fold each side of tortilla in, then roll up. Cut each in half to serve.

Yield: 6 servings, ½ wrap each
Meal Component: Meat/Meat Alternate, Grain, Fruit

Nutrition and Fitness Notes

Read books and show photographs that reflect the various food choices and practices of children and families in the program and in the larger community. Add related models and props to the dramatic play interest area.

The Experienced Provider

Family, community, and culture are fundamental to developing a strong identity as children come to understand where and how they belong and how they can contribute to the world. It is in this nurturing community that knowledge is constructed and traditions and ways of being are shared. How could your program's practices, rituals, and traditions cultivate a sense of belonging and encourage meaningful contributions in your program?

Activities for Children

Storytelling
Invite families who speak different languages (whether it is different varieties of English such as African American Language [AAL] or languages such as Mandarin or Arabic) to come and tell a story to the young learners. The children hear the language varieties used in the stories, which helps normalize the idea of language diversity.

Language College
Ask families and children how they greet someone who is a close friend or relative and then write those greetings on butcher paper. Read aloud the expressions to the students, then hand out magazines and art materials for the children to create a language collage together.

Greetings!
Foster adult-child relationships by including culturally specific greetings, like popular dances, handshakes, and gestures from movies or television shows, and singing culturally responsive songs, nursery rhymes, and chants.

Literacy Corner

Global Babies by The Global Fund for Children
With vibrant color photographs, this board book gives glimpses into the daily life, traditions, and clothing of babies from around the world.

Amy Wu and the Warm Welcome by Kat Zhang
When new student Lin arrives in their class, Amy Wu tries to include him, but Lin doesn't speak. When she sees him chatting with his family in Chinese, she forms a plan to help him feel at home.

JANUARY ATTENDANCE AND PAYMENT LOG

To record drop-off and pickup times that vary, try using two lines per child.

CHILD'S NAME	S	M 1	T 2	W 3	T 4	F	S	TOTAL	S 5	M 6	T 7	W 8	T 9	F 10	S 11	TOTAL	S 12	M 13	T 14	W 15	T 16	F 17	S 18	TOTAL	S 19	M 20	T 21	W 22	T 23	F 24	S 25	TOTAL	S 26	M 27	T 28	W 29	T 30	F 31	S	TOTAL	S	M

JANUARY ATTENDANCE AND PAYMENT LOG CONTINUED

CHILD'S NAME	S	M	T	W 1	T 2	F 3	S 4	TOTAL	S 5	M 6	T 7	W 8	T 9	F 10	S 11	TOTAL	S 12	M 13	T 14	W 15	T 16	F 17	S 18	TOTAL	S 19	M 20	T 21	W 22	T 23	F 24	S 25	TOTAL	S 26	M 27	T 28	W 29	T 30	F 31	TOTAL	S	M

WEEKLY PAYMENT TOTALS

	FOOD PROGRAM INCOME RECVD	PARENT FEE INCOME RECVD	OTHER INCOME RECVD			
JANUARY INCOME*				=	JAN TOTAL	
BALANCE FORWARD				=	BALANCE FWD TOTAL	
TOTAL Y-T-D INCOME				=	TOTAL Y-T-D	

Food Program Claim

Date Claim Sent _____

Date Check Received _____

MEAL COUNT TALLY

BREAKFASTS	
LUNCHES	
DINNERS	
SNACKS	

*Include income received in January 2025 for meals served in 2024.

Put totals in year-end meal tally, page 95.

JANUARY EXPENSE REPORT

DATE	PAYMENT TYPE cash, check #, cc #, debit	PURCHASED FROM	PURCHASE TOTAL	ADVERTISING	INSURANCE	INTEREST	LEGAL & PROFESSIONAL SERVICES	OFFICE EXPENSES (including internet & 2nd phone)	RENT OF BUSINESS PROPERTY	REPAIR & MAINTENANCE	SUPPLIES		MILES
		THIS MONTH'S TOTAL											
		BALANCE CARRIED FORWARD											
		YEAR-TO-DATE TOTAL											

JANUARY EXPENSE REPORT

DATE	PAYMENT TYPE cash, check #, cc #, debit	PURCHASED FROM	PURCHASE TOTAL	TAXES & LICENSES	TRAVEL & ENTERTAINMENT	FOOD	TOYS	HOUSEHOLD ITEMS	CLEANING SUPPLIES	ACTIVITY EXPENSES			MILES
			THIS MONTH'S TOTAL										
			BALANCE CARRIED FORWARD										
			YEAR-TO-DATE TOTAL										

See page 85 for an explanation of how to transfer expenses to your tax forms. You may wish to relabel the columns to fit your business needs.

See page 6 for an explanation of the order in which we present the categories.

FEBRUARY 2025

	Hours Worked
	Previous Total
	No. Hours Open*
	Other Hours Worked**
	Year-to-Date Total

* "No. Hours Open" refers to hours from when the first child arrived to when the last child left (not your advertised work hours).
** "Other Hours Worked" refers to hours spent on business activities in the home (cleaning, meal preparation, activity planning, and so on) when children are not present.

SUN	MON	TUE	WED	THU	FRI	SAT
JANUARY 2025	MARCH 2025					**1** Black History Month Dental Health Month
2 Groundhog Day	**3** Fire Drill Day	**4**	**5**	**6**	**7**	**8**
9	**10**	**11**	**12** Severe Storm Drill Day	**13**	**14** Valentine's Day	**15**
16	**17** Presidents' Day	**18**	**19**	**20**	**21**	**22**
23	**24**	**25**	**26**	**27**	**28** Call your local R & R agency; update your service	

FEBRUARY

I Love Myself

I rest, eat well, breathe deep, and play,
Giving me care and love each day.

Recipes

Berry and Quinoa Breakfast Bake

¼ cup dry quinoa, rinsed
½ cup rolled oats
2 tablespoons brown sugar
¼ teaspoon cinnamon
⅛ teaspoon salt
1¼ cups milk
¼ teaspoon vanilla extract
3 cups mixed frozen berries

1. Preheat oven to 400° F. Grease a loaf pan.
2. In a medium bowl, combine quinoa, oats, brown sugar, cinnamon, salt, milk, vanilla extract, and berries. Mix well. Pour mixture into prepared loaf pan.
3. Bake for 25–30 minutes or until quinoa is cooked. Remove from the oven and stir carefully. Serve hot, or chill to serve cold.

Yield: 6 servings, ½ cup each
Meal Component: Grain, Fruit

Grilled Ham, Cheese, and Tomato Sandwiches

1 teaspoon margarine, melted
6 slices whole wheat bread, at least 1 ounce each
6 slices reduced-fat Swiss cheese
6 slices fresh tomato
4½ slices reduced-sodium deli ham

1. Preheat oven to 350° F.
2. Lightly brush melted margarine onto one side of each piece of bread. Place 1 slice of cheese, 2 slices of tomato, and 1½ slices of ham onto unbuttered sides of 3 slices of bread. Top with the additional slices of cheese and bread, buttered sides facing out.
3. Place sandwiches on a baking sheet. Bake in the oven for 10–12 minutes or until cheese is melted and bread is lightly toasted. Cut in half to serve.

Yield: 3 sandwiches, ½ sandwich per serving
Meal Component: Meat/Meat Alternate, Grain

Serving sizes are for ages 3–5. Guidelines for the proper credit of food may vary in some states. Please check with the CACFP in your state for more information.

Menu of the Month

Breakfast
Milk
Berry and Quinoa Breakfast Bake* (WG)

Morning Snack
Water
Whole Wheat Pita
Peanut Butter

Lunch
Milk
Grilled Ham, Cheese, and Tomato Sandwiches* (WG)
Mango Chunks
Steamed Snow Peas

Afternoon Snack
100% Apple Juice
Graham Crackers

*Indicates recipes of the month.
(WG) Indicates whole grain
Recipes adapted from the Institute of Childhood Nutrition.

Nutrition and Fitness Notes

Serve meals and snacks family style, helping children learn to serve themselves and encouraging them to try new foods. Create a pleasant and appealing environment during mealtimes, with conversations centered on children's interests.

The Experienced Provider

As early childhood professionals, our own needs are often subjugated by the demands placed on us. Our profession speaks of well-being as something that we do for the children's sake—we need to take care of ourselves so that we can take care of others. But you are worthy of being well and being in care of yourself. Period. On the many paths to well-being, practice self-compassion and care of self. Be attentive to your needs while holding awareness of others'.

Activities for Children

Describing Me
Invite children to create a self-portrait of themselves doing something they love to do. When they have completed their portraits, ask them to choose one word to describe themselves and write it on their artwork (with adult assistance as needed).

Rest and Rejuvenation
Most young children need to rest or relax at some time during the day. Without adult guidance to rest, children may become exhausted, overstimulated, or stressed without being aware of how they are feeling. Physical exhaustion and overstimulation increase stress, and the resulting change in a child's energy level is often misjudged by adults and treated as misbehavior. Helping children learn to recognize when they are tired or stressed and teaching them how to rest or relax may help reduce inappropriate behaviors and, in some cases, physical illnesses.

Supportive Conversations
We support positive identity development and encourage appreciation and accurate language for differences when we notice and include experiences and conversations about the children and their families as a part of our everyday lives.

Literacy Corner

The Colors of Us by Karen Katz
Through the eyes of a little girl who begins to see her familiar world in a new way, this book celebrates the differences and similarities that connect all people.

You Are Important by Todd Snow
This warm, affirming book helps children know they matter because they are growing and learning new things, because they smile and laugh, and because we get to hug them.

FEBRUARY ATTENDANCE AND PAYMENT LOG

To record drop-off and pickup times that vary, try using two lines per child.

CHILD'S NAME	S	M	T	W	T	F	S 1	TOTAL	S 2	M 3	T 4	W 5	T 6	F 7	S 8	TOTAL	S 9	M 10	T 11	W 12	T 13	F 14	S 15	TOTAL	S 16	M 17	T 18	W 19	T 20	F 21	S 22	TOTAL	S 23	M 24	T 25	W 26	T 27	F 28	TOTAL	S	M

FEBRUARY ATTENDANCE AND PAYMENT LOG CONTINUED

CHILD'S NAME	S	M	T	W	T	F	S 1	TOTAL	S 2	M 3	T 4	W 5	T 6	F 7	S 8	TOTAL	S 9	M 10	T 11	W 12	T 13	F 14	S 15	TOTAL	S 16	M 17	T 18	W 19	T 20	F 21	S 22	TOTAL	S 23	M 24	T 25	W 26	T 27	F 28	S	TOTAL	S	M

WEEKLY PAYMENT TOTALS

	FOOD PROGRAM INCOME RECVD	PARENT FEE INCOME RECVD	OTHER INCOME RECVD			
FEBRUARY INCOME				=	FEB TOTAL	
BALANCE FORWARD				=	BALANCE FWD TOTAL	
TOTAL Y-T-D INCOME				=	TOTAL Y-T-D	

Food Program Claim

Date Claim Sent _____

Date Check Received _____

MEAL COUNT TALLY

BREAKFASTS	
LUNCHES	
DINNERS	
SNACKS	

Put totals in year-end meal tally, page 95.

FEBRUARY EXPENSE REPORT

DATE	PAYMENT TYPE cash, check #, cc #, debit	PURCHASED FROM	PURCHASE TOTAL	ADVERTISING	INSURANCE	INTEREST	LEGAL & PROFESSIONAL SERVICES	OFFICE EXPENSES (including internet & 2nd phone)	RENT OF BUSINESS PROPERTY	REPAIR & MAINTENANCE	SUPPLIES		MILES
		THIS MONTH'S TOTAL											
		BALANCE CARRIED FORWARD											
		YEAR-TO-DATE TOTAL											

FEBRUARY EXPENSE REPORT

DATE	PAYMENT TYPE cash, check #, cc #, debit	PURCHASED FROM	PURCHASE TOTAL	TAXES & LICENSES	TRAVEL & ENTERTAINMENT	FOOD	TOYS	HOUSEHOLD ITEMS	CLEANING SUPPLIES	ACTIVITY EXPENSES			MILES
		THIS MONTH'S TOTAL											
		BALANCE CARRIED FORWARD											
		YEAR-TO-DATE TOTAL											

See page 85 for an explanation of how to transfer expenses to your tax forms. You may wish to relabel the columns to fit your business needs.

See page 6 for an explanation of the order in which we present the categories.

MARCH 2025

	Hours Worked
	Previous Total
	No. Hours Open*
	Other Hours Worked**
	Year-to-Date Total

* "No. Hours Open" refers to hours from when the first child arrived to when the last child left (not your advertised work hours).
** "Other Hours Worked" refers to hours spent on business activities in the home (cleaning, meal preparation, activity planning, and so on) when children are not present.

SUN	MON	TUE	WED	THU	FRI	SAT
FEBRUARY 2025 / APRIL 2025						**1** National Women's History Month / National Nutrition Month / National Reading Month / Ramadan begins (Islamic)
2 Read Across America Day	**3** Fire Drill Day	**4** Mardi Gras	**5** Ash Wednesday (Christian)	**6**	**7**	**8**
9	**10**	**11**	**12** Severe Storm Drill Day	**13**	**14** Purim (Jewish)	**15**
16	**17** St. Patrick's Day	**18**	**19**	**20** Spring begins / Change your smoke alarms and carbon monoxide filter batteries	**21**	**22**
23	**24**	**25**	**26**	**27**	**28** Good Friday (Christian) / Call your local R & R agency; update your service	**29**
30 Ramadan ends (Islamic)	**31** Eid al-Fitr (Islamic)					

MARCH

Learning with Our Senses

Hear and see, touch, taste, and smell,
I learn what all my senses tell.

Recipes

Cinnamon-Citrus French Toast

2 teaspoons margarine, melted
2 tablespoons maple syrup
½ teaspoon ground cinnamon
1 egg
¼ cup frozen 100% orange juice concentrate, thawed
2 tablespoons milk
3 slices whole wheat bread, at least 1 ounce each, torn into medium-sized pieces

1. Preheat oven to 375° F. Grease a loaf pan.
2. In a medium bowl, use a hand mixer to mix margarine, maple syrup, cinnamon, egg, orange juice concentrate, and milk. Toss with bread pieces.
3. Spread evenly into loaf pan. Bake for 25 minutes or until golden brown. Cut into six squares.

Yield: 6 servings, one square each
Meal Component: Grain

Chicken and Cheese Snack Cup with Grapes

3 ounces cooked rotisserie chicken breast, diced
6 tablespoons Colby cheese, diced into ¼-inch cubes
3 cups seedless red grapes, washed and cut in half

1. Layer chicken and cheese into six 6-ounce clear plastic cups (1 tablespoon chicken and 1 tablespoon cheese). Top each cup with ½ cup sliced grapes.

Yield: 6 servings
Meal Component: Meat/Meat Alternate, Fruit

Serving sizes are for ages 3–5. Guidelines for the proper credit of food may vary in some states. Please check with the CACFP in your state for more information.

Menu of the Month

Breakfast
Milk
Cinnamon-Citrus French Toast* (WG)
Grapes

Morning Snack
Water
Pear Slices
Whole Grain Granola (WG)

Lunch
Milk
Turkey Burgers
Whole Wheat Bun
Green Beans
Canned Mixed Fruit

Afternoon Snack
Water
Chicken and Cheese Snack Cup with Grapes*

*Indicates recipes of the month.
(WG) Indicates whole grain
Recipes adapted from the Institute of Childhood Nutrition.

Nutrition and Fitness Notes

Young children will not know and do not need to understand which nutrients are in specific foods. They do need to develop an appreciation for the wide variety of foods available. By eating foods in a variety of colors, textures, temperatures, and tastes, most children will consume the nutrients they need for healthful growth and development.

The Experienced Provider

Young children need to interact with materials, experiment, and observe the results. Preschoolers and kindergartners are still determining the difference between reality and fantasy. By observing a classroom goldfish, children may notice that it does not behave like the fish in storybooks. While a car viewed in a cartoon may jump vertically or fly through the air, the cars that children roll down ramps behave in consistent, predictable ways.

Activities for Children

Wet Sponge Dry Sponge
Let children try to wipe up a spill with a dry sponge and then a moist sponge. The moist sponge is much more effective in wiping up the spill, because liquids can move against gravity to occupy the small spaces between fibers, a process called capillary action. Water also has a strong cohesive property, which means that it tends to grab hold of other water molecules. Since the moist sponge already has water in it, this water pulls the new liquid into the sponge. Have children place a moist sponge on one section of the spill and a dry sponge on another and count to 10, then check which absorbed the most liquid. Children can use several methods: (1) compare which sponge left more of the spill, (2) squeeze both sponges into the sink and see which releases more liquid, and (3) hold both sponges to determine which feels heavier and is therefore holding more liquid.

Guess the Smell
Provide children with something to cover their eyes, such as a blindfold, and invite them to try to guess a smell placed under their nose. Alternatively, place something within a sensory box that children cannot see inside and have them guess what it is by smell.

Noticing Differences
Many people think that children don't notice differences and believe that bringing up differences grows prejudice and racism. In fact, the opposite is true. Children begin to notice differences between themselves and other people when they are babies, and research shows that they begin to show a preference for people who look like them as early as three months of age.

Literacy Corner

Quiet! by Kate Alizadeh
The text and sensory clues in this inclusive picture book allow children to experience their home through the many noises it makes.

Baby Loves the Five Senses: Sight! by Ruth Spiro
Accurate enough for experts yet simple enough for baby, this board book explores the science of vision, light, and color.

MARCH ATTENDANCE AND PAYMENT LOG

To record drop-off and pickup times that vary, try using two lines per child.

CHILD'S NAME	S	M	T	W	T	F	S 1	TOTAL	S 2	M 3	T 4	W 5	T 6	F 7	S 8	TOTAL	S 9	M 10	T 11	W 12	T 13	F 14	S 15	TOTAL	S 16	M 17	T 18	W 19	T 20	F 21	S 22	TOTAL	S 23	M 24	T 25	W 26	T 27	F 28	S 29	TOTAL	S 30	M 31	

MARCH ATTENDANCE AND PAYMENT LOG CONTINUED

CHILD'S NAME	S 1	M	T	W	T	F	S	TOTAL	S 2	M 3	T 4	W 5	T 6	F 7	S 8	TOTAL	S 9	M 10	T 11	W 12	T 13	F 14	S 15	TOTAL	S 16	M 17	T 18	W 19	T 20	F 21	S 22	TOTAL	S 23	M 24	T 25	W 26	T 27	F 28	S 29	TOTAL	S 30	M 31

WEEKLY PAYMENT TOTALS

	FOOD PROGRAM INCOME RECVD	PARENT FEE INCOME RECVD	OTHER INCOME RECVD			
MARCH INCOME				=	MAR TOTAL	
BALANCE FORWARD				=	BALANCE FWD TOTAL	
TOTAL Y-T-D INCOME				=	TOTAL Y-T-D	

Food Program Claim

Date Claim Sent _____

Date Check Received _____

MEAL COUNT TALLY

BREAKFASTS	
LUNCHES	
DINNERS	
SNACKS	

Put totals in year-end meal tally, page 95.

MARCH EXPENSE REPORT

DATE	PAYMENT TYPE cash, check #, cc #, debit	PURCHASED FROM	PURCHASE TOTAL	ADVERTISING	INSURANCE	INTEREST	LEGAL & PROFESSIONAL SERVICES	OFFICE EXPENSES (including internet & 2nd phone)	RENT OF BUSINESS PROPERTY	REPAIR & MAINTENANCE	SUPPLIES		MILES
		THIS MONTH'S TOTAL											
		BALANCE CARRIED FORWARD											
		YEAR-TO-DATE TOTAL											

MARCH EXPENSE REPORT

DATE	PAYMENT TYPE cash, check #, cc #, debit	PURCHASED FROM	PURCHASE TOTAL	TAXES & LICENSES	TRAVEL & ENTERTAINMENT	FOOD	TOYS	HOUSEHOLD ITEMS	CLEANING SUPPLIES	ACTIVITY EXPENSES			MILES
		THIS MONTH'S TOTAL											
		BALANCE CARRIED FORWARD											
		YEAR-TO-DATE TOTAL											

See page 85 for an explanation of how to transfer expenses to your tax forms. You may wish to relabel the columns to fit your business needs.

See page 6 for an explanation of the order in which we present the categories.

APRIL 2025

	Hours Worked
	Previous Total
	No. Hours Open*
	Other Hours Worked**
	Year-to-Date Total

* "No. Hours Open" refers to hours from when the first child arrived to when the last child left (not your advertised work hours).

** "Other Hours Worked" refers to hours spent on business activities in the home (cleaning, meal preparation, activity planning, and so on) when children are not present.

SUN	MON	TUE	WED	THU	FRI	SAT
		1 April Fools' Day / National Child Abuse Prevention Month	**2**	**3**	**4**	**5**
6	**7** Week of the Young Child / Fire Drill Day	**8**	**9** Severe Storm Drill Day	**10** National Siblings Day	**11**	**12**
13 Palm Sunday (Christian) / Passover begins (Jewish)	**14**	**15** 2024 income taxes due / 2025 1st quarter estimated taxes due	**16**	**17**	**18**	**19** Patriots' Day
20 Easter Sunday (Christian) / Passover ends (Jewish) / Orthodox Easter (Orthodox)	**21**	**22** Earth Day	**23**	**24**	**25** Arbor Day	**26**
27	**28**	**29**	**30** Call your local R & R agency; update your service			

MARCH 2025

S	M	T	W	T	F	S
						1
2	3	4	5	6	7	8
9	10	11	12	13	14	15
16	17	18	19	20	21	22
23	24	25	26	27	28	29
30	31					

MAY 2025

S	M	T	W	T	F	S
				1	2	3
4	5	6	7	8	9	10
11	12	13	14	15	16	17
18	19	20	21	22	23	24
25	26	27	28	29	30	31

APRIL

Welcome Spring!
Trees bud, birds chirp, spring comes alive,
We go outside, it helps us thrive.

Recipes

Fish and Veggie Packets
13½ ounces flounder fish fillets, thawed (fresh or frozen, each piece should be about 3 ounces)
1 teaspoon garlic and herb salt-free seasoning
1 tablespoon margarine, melted
2¾ cups frozen mixed cauliflower and broccoli florets

1. Preheat oven to 400° F.
2. Cut 6 pieces of parchment paper into 8-by-12-inch squares. Fold each square in half. In the center, next to the folded seam, place 1 piece of fish.
3. Add the seasoning to the melted margarine. In a medium bowl, combine vegetables and seasoned margarine. Toss to mix.
4. Place ½ cup of seasoned vegetables on top of each piece of fish. Roll and then fold the edges of the parchment paper together to create a packet. Place fish packets on a baking sheet. Bake for 25 minutes, until the internal temperature of the fish reaches 145° F.

Yield: 6 packets, one packet per serving
Meal Component: Meat/Meat Alternate, Vegetable

Parmesan Zucchini Chips
½ cup whole wheat breadcrumbs
½ teaspoon Italian seasoning
1½ tablespoons grated Parmesan cheese
5 cups sliced fresh zucchini
¼ cup reduced-fat mayonnaise

1. Preheat oven to 400° F. Line baking sheets with foil or parchment paper and spray with nonstick cooking spray.
2. In a small bowl, combine breadcrumbs, Italian seasoning, and Parmesan cheese.
3. In a separate bowl, combine zucchini rounds and mayonnaise. Add breadcrumb mixture and stir until all rounds are coated.
4. Place zucchini rounds in a single layer on prepared baking sheet. Sprinkle any remaining breadcrumb mixture on top. Bake until golden brown and crispy, about 20 minutes.

Yield: 6 servings, ½ cup each
Meal Component: Vegetable

Menu of the Month

Breakfast
Milk
Whole Wheat Toast (WG)
Blueberries

Morning Snack
Water
Cucumber Spears
Hummus

Lunch
Milk
Fish and Veggie Packets*
Whole Wheat Roll (WG)
Cantaloupe Chunks

Afternoon Snack
Water
Parmesan Zucchini Chips*
Cottage Cheese

*Indicates recipes of the month.
(WG) Indicates whole grain
Recipes adapted from the Institute of Childhood Nutrition.

Nutrition and Fitness Notes

Active play is essential to optimal physical development, fitness, and the overall health of young children. The benefits of active physical play throughout the day are many: increased physical development and fitness, improved weight management, increased self-esteem, and enhanced learning readiness, among many others.

The Experienced Provider

We often want our program to be fabulous immediately. Remember it takes time to create a rich environment. The best early childhood environments are continually evolving according to children's interests, abilities, and needs. Know that everything does not need to be done right away. Take time and gradually add interesting finds from weekend expeditions and garage sales.

Activities for Children

What Grows Above and Below Ground?
Help children plant seeds for green beans, carrots, lettuce, and onions in a clear plastic container that is narrow but relatively deep (plant them close to the edge of the box). Many children do not realize that important parts of plants are also under the ground. Ask: Do all of the plants have roots? Do the tops of the plants look the same or different? Do the roots of the plants look the same or different? Which plant has the longest root? Provide magnifying glasses, journals for children to note their observations, and rulers, as well as nonstandard measurement tools such as blocks or paper clips.

Picnic Time
Ask children to tell you what they know about picnics, and involve them in planning one. With children, plan a picnic for the dolls and toy people. Together, list all the things you would need for a picnic. Count the dolls and toy people, and conduct an inventory of the pretend food available to determine if more is needed.

Equity for All
Equality works if everyone's needs are the same. Equity works when people's diverse needs are met. Equity, not equality, is about fairness and justice. Check out this blog post for help on how to explain equity and equality to young children: https://bit.ly/2PWyurf.

Literacy Corner

Planting a Rainbow by Lois Ehlert
With bold collage illustrations, this book helps children understand how to plant bulbs, seeds, and seedlings, and nurture their growth.

Birdsong by Julie Flett
This story of the friendship between Katherena and her elderly neighbor highlights intergenerational relationships, shared passions, and spending time outdoors with loved ones.

Serving sizes are for ages 3–5. Guidelines for the proper credit of food may vary in some states. Please check with the CACFP in your state for more information.

APRIL ATTENDANCE AND PAYMENT LOG

To record drop-off and pickup times that vary, try using two lines per child.

CHILD'S NAME	S	M 1	T 2	W 3	T 4	F 5	S	TOTAL	S 6	M 7	T 8	W 9	T 10	F 11	S 12	TOTAL	S 13	M 14	T 15	W 16	T 17	F 18	S 19	TOTAL	S 20	M 21	T 22	W 23	T 24	F 25	S 26	TOTAL	S 27	M 28	T 29	W 30	T	F	S	TOTAL	S	M

APRIL ATTENDANCE AND PAYMENT LOG CONTINUED

CHILD'S NAME	S	M T W T F	S	TOTAL	S	M T W T F	S	TOTAL	S	M T W T F	S	TOTAL	S	M T W T F	S	TOTAL	S	M T W T F		TOTAL	S	M
		1 2 3 4	5		6	7 8 9 10 11	12		13	14 15 16 17 18	19		20	21 22 23 24 25	26		27	28 29 30				

WEEKLY PAYMENT TOTALS

	FOOD PROGRAM INCOME RECVD	PARENT FEE INCOME RECVD	OTHER INCOME RECVD			
APRIL INCOME				=	APR TOTAL	
BALANCE FORWARD				=	BALANCE FWD TOTAL	
TOTAL Y-T-D INCOME				=	TOTAL Y-T-D	

Food Program Claim

Date Claim Sent _____

Date Check Received _____

MEAL COUNT TALLY

BREAKFASTS	
LUNCHES	
DINNERS	
SNACKS	

Put totals in year-end meal tally, page 95.

APRIL EXPENSE REPORT

DATE	PAYMENT TYPE cash, check #, cc #, debit	PURCHASED FROM	PURCHASE TOTAL	ADVERTISING	INSURANCE	INTEREST	LEGAL & PROFESSIONAL SERVICES	OFFICE EXPENSES (including internet & 2nd phone)	RENT OF BUSINESS PROPERTY	REPAIR & MAINTENANCE	SUPPLIES		MILES
		THIS MONTH'S TOTAL											
		BALANCE CARRIED FORWARD											
		YEAR-TO-DATE TOTAL											

APRIL EXPENSE REPORT

DATE	PAYMENT TYPE cash, check #, cc #, debit	PURCHASED FROM	PURCHASE TOTAL	TAXES & LICENSES	TRAVEL & ENTERTAINMENT	FOOD	TOYS	HOUSEHOLD ITEMS	CLEANING SUPPLIES	ACTIVITY EXPENSES			MILES
		THIS MONTH'S TOTAL											
		BALANCE CARRIED FORWARD											
		YEAR-TO-DATE TOTAL											

See page 85 for an explanation of how to transfer expenses to your tax forms.
You may wish to relabel the columns to fit your business needs.

See page 6 for an explanation of the order in which we present the categories.

MAY 2025

					Hours Worked	
					Previous Total	
					No. Hours Open*	
					Other Hours Worked**	
					Year-to-Date Total	

* "No. Hours Open" refers to hours from when the first child arrived to when the last child left (not your advertised work hours).
** "Other Hours Worked" refers to hours spent on business activities in the home (cleaning, meal preparation, activity planning, and so on) when children are not present.

SUN	MON	TUE	WED	THU	FRI	SAT
APRIL 2025 / JUNE 2025				**1** Physical Fitness and Sports Month — May Day	**2**	**3**
4	**5** Cinco de Mayo — Fire Drill Day	**6** National Teacher Day	**7**	**8**	**9** Provider Appreciation Day	**10**
11 Mother's Day	**12**	**13**	**14** Severe Storm Drill Day	**15**	**16**	**17**
18	**19**	**20**	**21**	**22**	**23**	**24**
25 National Missing Children's Day	**26** Memorial Day	**27**	**28**	**29**	**30** Call your local R & R agency; update your service	**31**

MAY

Art Around Us
Color and form and shape and line,
Wherever I look I see art so fine.

Recipes

Deli Bento Box
¼ cup reduced-fat mayonnaise
1 tablespoon yellow mustard
1 tablespoon honey
¼ teaspoon garlic powder
3 slices low-sodium deli turkey
3 slices reduced-fat cheddar cheese (1 ounce each)
12 grape tomatoes
¾ cup cucumber slices
18 woven whole wheat crackers

1. In a small bowl, whisk together mayonnaise, mustard, honey, and garlic powder.
2. Cut turkey slices in half. Cut each slice of cheese into quarters.
3. In six bento boxes with four chambers, place in each ⅙ of the dressing, 2 pieces of cheese and 1 piece of turkey, 2 grape tomatoes and 2 cucumber slices, and 3 crackers.

Yield: 6 servings, one bento box each
Meal Component: Meat/Meat Alternate, Grain, Vegetable

Barbecue Beef Sliders
14½ ounces beef chuck roast, without bone, practically free of fat
¼ cup barbecue sauce
6 whole wheat rolls or slider buns

1. Place beef in a slow cooker, at least 2 quarts. Cook on low for 4 hours or cook on high for 2 hours. Heat to an internal temperature of 145° F.
2. Place beef on a cutting board. Use two forks to shred beef into strips.
3. In a medium bowl, combine shredded beef, barbecue sauce, and 2 tablespoons of au jus (liquid) from the slow cooker. Place ¼ cup barbecue beef between each roll.

Yield: 6 servings, one sandwich each
Meal Component: Meat/Meat Alternate, Grain

Menu of the Month

Breakfast
Milk
Stone-Ground Grits (WG)
Kiwi Slices

Morning Snack
Water
Deli Bento Box* (WG)

Lunch
Milk
Barbecue Beef Sliders* (WG)
Steamed Broccoli
Apple Slices

Afternoon Snack
Water
Yogurt
Baby Carrots

*Indicates recipes of the month.
(WG) Indicates whole grain
Recipes adapted from the Institute of Childhood Nutrition.

Nutrition and Fitness Notes

Foods that are familiar, that look and smell good, and that are served in child-size portions are generally more appetizing to children. Try preparing and offering foods in various and creative ways, such as slicing a bright red apple to reveal the "star" or offering plain or flavored yogurt, light dressing, or other dips with raw vegetables and fruits.

The Experienced Provider

Environments affect how we feel, think, and behave. Surrounding children and educators with aesthetically appealing loose parts in interesting textures, colors, and sounds enhances the beauty of play spaces. Consider the natural beauty of a collection of seashells, sea glass, and driftwood. The colors complement each other, and their textures beckon you to run your fingers over them. A bowl of buttons entices you to dive your hand in deep and pull out a fistful.

Activities for Children

Plant Imprints
Provide a variety of weeds, wildflowers, grasses, and other plants (use a smartphone app to ensure the plants aren't harmful). Guide children to sponge paint onto their plants. Talk about plant parts and why they are important to the plant. Carefully place another sheet of paper or a lightweight piece of cardboard over the plants. Children can roll brayers (paint rollers) over the top sheet to create paint impressions of the plants on the bottom paper. When dry, create a book showing a photo of each child's plant and the collage of imprints it created.

Parallel Line Art
Tape two markers together for children to instantly draw parallel straight lines. Even if children create loops with the markers, the two colors stay the same distance apart. As children experiment, talk about the lines the children are creating and point out parallel lines you can see, such as bookcase shelves. Photograph examples of parallel lines that children discover around them, then combine with the children's descriptions to create a book about parallel lines. At another time, a similar book can be created for lines that intersect.

Skin Tone Paint Mixing
Educators often use paint mixing as an entry point to talk about skin color and race. After children mix paint to make their skin tone and name their color, adults and children can have conversations about how colored racial terms (Black, White) describe people with a range of skin colors.

Literacy Corner

My Yellow Umbrella by Chris Robertson
Bright, retro-inspired illustrations accompany a little girl on her dreamy day with a yellow umbrella.

A Splash of Red: The Life and Art of Horace Pippin by Jen Bryant
This is the story of Horace Pippin, a self-taught painter from humble beginnings who despite many obstacles was ultimately recognized for who he was: an artist.

MAY ATTENDANCE AND PAYMENT LOG

To record drop-off and pickup times that vary, try using two lines per child.

CHILD'S NAME	S	M	T	W	T 1	F 2	S 3	TOTAL	S 4	M 5	T 6	W 7	T 8	F 9	S 10	TOTAL	S 11	M 12	T 13	W 14	T 15	F 16	S 17	TOTAL	S 18	M 19	T 20	W 21	T 22	F 23	S 24	TOTAL	S 25	M 26	T 27	W 28	T 29	F 30	S 31	TOTAL	S	M

MAY ATTENDANCE AND PAYMENT LOG CONTINUED

CHILD'S NAME	S	M	T	W	T	F	S	TOTAL	S	M	T	W	T	F	S	TOTAL	S	M	T	W	T	F	S	TOTAL	S	M	T	W	T	F	S	TOTAL	S	M	T	W	T	F	S	TOTAL	S	M
					1	2	3		4	5	6	7	8	9	10		11	12	13	14	15	16	17		18	19	20	21	22	23	24		25	26	27	28	29	30	31			

WEEKLY PAYMENT TOTALS

	FOOD PROGRAM INCOME RECVD	PARENT FEE INCOME RECVD	OTHER INCOME RECVD			
MAY INCOME				=	MAY TOTAL	
BALANCE FORWARD				=	BALANCE FWD TOTAL	
TOTAL Y-T-D INCOME				=	TOTAL Y-T-D	

Food Program Claim

Date Claim Sent _____

Date Check Received _____

MEAL COUNT TALLY

BREAKFASTS	
LUNCHES	
DINNERS	
SNACKS	

Put totals in year-end meal tally, page 95.

MAY EXPENSE REPORT

DATE	PAYMENT TYPE cash, check #, cc #, debit	PURCHASED FROM	PURCHASE TOTAL	ADVERTISING	INSURANCE	INTEREST	LEGAL & PROFESSIONAL SERVICES	OFFICE EXPENSES (including internet & 2nd phone)	RENT OF BUSINESS PROPERTY	REPAIR & MAINTENANCE	SUPPLIES		MILES
		THIS MONTH'S TOTAL											
		BALANCE CARRIED FORWARD											
		YEAR-TO-DATE TOTAL											

MAY EXPENSE REPORT

DATE	PAYMENT TYPE cash, check #, cc #, debit	PURCHASED FROM	PURCHASE TOTAL	TAXES & LICENSES	TRAVEL & ENTERTAINMENT	FOOD	TOYS	HOUSEHOLD ITEMS	CLEANING SUPPLIES	ACTIVITY EXPENSES			MILES
		THIS MONTH'S TOTAL											
		BALANCE CARRIED FORWARD											
		YEAR-TO-DATE TOTAL											

See page 85 for an explanation of how to transfer expenses to your tax forms. You may wish to relabel the columns to fit your business needs.

See page 6 for an explanation of the order in which we present the categories.

JUNE 2025

			Hours Worked	
			Previous Total	
			No. Hours Open*	
			Other Hours Worked**	
			Year-to-Date Total	

* "No. Hours Open" refers to hours from when the first child arrived to when the last child left (not your advertised work hours).

** "Other Hours Worked" refers to hours spent on business activities in the home (cleaning, meal preparation, activity planning, and so on) when children are not present.

SUN	MON	TUE	WED	THU	FRI	SAT
1	**2** Shavuot (Jewish) / Fire Drill Day	**3**	**4**	**5** Hajj begins (Islamic)	**6**	**7** Eid al-Adha (Islamic)
8 Pentecost (Christian)	**9**	**10**	**11** Severe Storm Drill Day	**12**	**13**	**14** Flag Day
15 Father's Day	**16** 2025 2nd quarter estimated taxes due	**17**	**18**	**19** Juneteenth	**20** Summer begins	**21**
22	**23**	**24**	**25**	**26**	**27** Islamic New Year	**28**
29	**30** Call your local R & R agency; update your service					

Replenish your stock of *Family Child Care Business Receipt Books, Inventory-Keepers,* and *Mileage-Keepers.*

MAY 2025
S	M	T	W	T	F	S
				1	2	3
4	5	6	7	8	9	10
11	12	13	14	15	16	17
18	19	20	21	22	23	24
25	26	27	28	29	30	31

JULY 2025
S	M	T	W	T	F	S
		1	2	3	4	5
6	7	8	9	10	11	12
13	14	15	16	17	18	19
20	21	22	23	24	25	26
27	28	29	30	31		

JUNE

Growing Big and Strong

Growing big and growing strong,
Healthy habits are lifelong!

Recipes

Chicken and Waffles with Maple-Peach Glaze
½ cup peach preserves
¼ cup maple syrup
13½ ounces raw chicken tenders
3 whole wheat waffles, at least 1 ounce each

1. To make maple-peach glaze: In a small microwave-safe bowl, combine peach preserves and maple syrup. Heat in microwave for 30 seconds. Stir. Heat for 30 more seconds or until glaze begins to bubble around the sides and is well blended.
2. Heat a medium nonstick skillet on medium-high heat. Brown both sides of chicken tenders for 5 minutes. Reduce heat to medium. Cover. Cook for 7–8 minutes. Heat to an internal temperature of 165° F. If needed, turn tenders to prevent overbrowning.
3. Drizzle half of the maple-peach glaze over chicken. Decrease heat to low. Cover. Cook chicken for 3 minutes or until glaze begins to bubble.
4. Place waffles in toaster. Toast for 3 to 4 minutes. Serve 1 chicken tender with ½ waffle and 1 tablespoon of maple-peach glaze.

Yield: 6 servings
Meal Component: Meat/Meat Alternate, Grain

Corny Salsa with Tortilla Chips
2 cups frozen corn, thawed and drained
¾ cup diced fresh tomatoes
¾ cup diced cucumbers
2 tablespoons chopped green onions
½ teaspoon chili lime seasoning
2 tablespoons light sour cream
3 ounces tortilla chips

1. In a medium bowl, combine corn, tomatoes, cucumbers, green onions, chili lime seasoning, and sour cream. Stir to mix. Serve ½ cup salsa and ½ ounce tortilla chips (about 5–7 chips).

Yield: 6 servings
Meal Component: Grain, Vegetable

Menu of the Month

Breakfast
Milk
Whole Wheat Bagels (WG)
Pitted Cherries

Morning Snack
Water
String Cheese
Mixed Berries

Lunch
Milk
Chicken and Waffles with Maple-Peach Glaze* (WG)
Mashed Sweet Potatoes
Nectarines

Afternoon Snack
Water
Corny Salsa with Tortilla Chips*

*Indicates recipes of the month.
(WG) Indicates whole grain
Recipes adapted from the Institute of Childhood Nutrition.

Nutrition and Fitness Notes

It is essential for children—and adults—to recognize that different foods help our bodies in different ways. Encourage children to eat a variety of foods to obtain adequate nutrients for growth and development. Whereas adults may use terms such as *nutrients*, children may better understand the concept of nutrition through description: foods can help them grow, give them energy to run and play, and help them become strong.

The Experienced Provider

Young children are naturally active, learning through movement and play. Many children love to run, jump, and climb, and if encouraged, they will naturally get plenty of physical activity, building a foundation for lifelong habits. Some children, however, may need more encouragement and assistance in order to participate in movement activities.

Activities for Children

Large Loose Parts
Play with large loose parts such as tires, crates, long planks, and heavy rocks fosters large-motor development. These play experiences are typically outdoors. Children use large-motor skills for transporting, arranging, stacking, rolling, constructing, deconstructing, and balancing. Muscle strength is needed to push, pull, move, and position heavy tires and to build big structures for climbing and balancing. Large loose parts allow children freedom to move materials and redesign spaces while fostering gross-motor skills.

Measuring Height
Have each child cut a piece of yarn that is the same height as they are. Then tape each piece in one part of the room, labeled with each child's name. The children can use nonstandard measuring tools such as blocks, paper clips, pumpkins, markers, and so on to measure how tall they are and then compare the heights of the others in the classroom. Children can try arranging the yarn from shortest to tallest and then tallest to shortest. Talk about how people are different in many ways and that these differences make life interesting and make us all individuals.

Forming Positive Self-Beliefs
Use art, children's books, and nature as springboards for countering negative beliefs about dark skin tones. These examples are a start to having open discussions about race.

Literacy Corner

I Will Dance by Nancy Bo Flood
This uplifting picture book follows a young girl born with cerebral palsy as she pursues her dream of becoming a dancer.

Beginners Are Brave by Rachel Robertson
Tommy tries something he has always wanted to do—play the tuba—and learns that some things take practice.

Serving sizes are for ages 3–5. Guidelines for the proper credit of food may vary in some states. Please check with the CACFP in your state for more information.

JUNE ATTENDANCE AND PAYMENT LOG

To record drop-off and pickup times that vary, try using two lines per child.

CHILD'S NAME	S 1	M 2	T 3	W 4	T 5	F 6	S 7	TOTAL	S 8	M 9	T 10	W 11	T 12	F 13	S 14	TOTAL	S 15	M 16	T 17	W 18	T 19	F 20	S 21	TOTAL	S 22	M 23	T 24	W 25	T 26	F 27	S 28	TOTAL	S 29	M 30	T	W	T	F	S	TOTAL	S	M

JUNE ATTENDANCE AND PAYMENT LOG CONTINUED

CHILD'S NAME	S 1	M 2	T 3	W 4	T 5	F 6	S 7	TOTAL	S 8	M 9	T 10	W 11	T 12	F 13	S 14	TOTAL	S 15	M 16	T 17	W 18	T 19	F 20	S 21	TOTAL	S 22	M 23	T 24	W 25	T 26	F 27	S 28	TOTAL	S 29	M 30	T	W	T	F	S	TOTAL	S	M

WEEKLY PAYMENT TOTALS

	FOOD PROGRAM INCOME RECVD	PARENT FEE INCOME RECVD	OTHER INCOME RECVD			
JUNE INCOME				=	JUN TOTAL	
BALANCE FORWARD				=	BALANCE FWD TOTAL	
TOTAL Y-T-D INCOME				=	TOTAL Y-T-D	

Food Program Claim

Date Claim Sent _____

Date Check Received _____

MEAL COUNT TALLY

BREAKFASTS	
LUNCHES	
DINNERS	
SNACKS	

Put totals in year-end meal tally, page 95.

JUNE EXPENSE REPORT

DATE	PAYMENT TYPE cash, check #, cc #, debit	PURCHASED FROM	PURCHASE TOTAL	ADVERTISING	INSURANCE	INTEREST	LEGAL & PROFESSIONAL SERVICES	OFFICE EXPENSES (including internet & 2nd phone)	RENT OF BUSINESS PROPERTY	REPAIR & MAINTENANCE	SUPPLIES		MILES
		THIS MONTH'S TOTAL											
		BALANCE CARRIED FORWARD											
		YEAR-TO-DATE TOTAL											

JUNE EXPENSE REPORT

DATE	PAYMENT TYPE cash, check #, cc #, debit	PURCHASED FROM	PURCHASE TOTAL	TAXES & LICENSES	TRAVEL & ENTERTAINMENT	FOOD	TOYS	HOUSEHOLD ITEMS	CLEANING SUPPLIES	ACTIVITY EXPENSES			MILES
			THIS MONTH'S TOTAL										
			BALANCE CARRIED FORWARD										
			YEAR-TO-DATE TOTAL										

See page 85 for an explanation of how to transfer expenses to your tax forms.
You may wish to relabel the columns to fit your business needs.

See page 6 for an explanation of the order in which we present the categories.

JULY 2025

Hours Worked	
Previous Total	
No. Hours Open*	
Other Hours Worked**	
Year-to-Date Total	

* "No. Hours Open" refers to hours from when the first child arrived to when the last child left (not your advertised work hours).
** "Other Hours Worked" refers to hours spent on business activities in the home (cleaning, meal preparation, activity planning, and so on) when children are not present.

SUN	MON	TUE	WED	THU	FRI	SAT
JUNE 2025	AUGUST 2025	1	2	3	4 Independence Day	5
6 Ashura (Islamic)	7 Fire Drill Day	8	9 Severe Storm Drill Day	10	11	12
13	14	15	16	17	18	19
20	21	22	23	24	25	26
27 Parents' Day	28	29	30 Friendship Day	31 Call your local R & R agency; update your service		

JULY

Bouncing and Rolling Balls
Tennis ball, beach ball, basketball—
We love to bounce and roll them all!

Recipes

Fruit and Yogurt Roll-Ups

¾ cup nonfat vanilla Greek yogurt
3 whole wheat tortillas, at least 1 ounce each
3 cups diced fresh strawberries
6 tablespoons granola, optional

1. Spread ¼ cup of yogurt on each tortilla. Top each tortilla with ½ cup strawberries. Sprinkle each tortilla with 1 tablespoon granola (optional).
2. Roll tortillas like a burrito. Cut in half on a bias (at an angle). Serve each with an additional ¼ cup of strawberries.

Yield: 6 servings
Meal Component: Grain, Fruit

Meatballs and Marinara

3 tablespoons instant brown rice, uncooked
1 egg
12 ounces 90% lean ground beef
1 teaspoon onion powder
½ teaspoon dried oregano
½ teaspoon Worcestershire sauce
1½ cups marinara sauce

1. Preheat oven to 400° F. In a small microwave-safe bowl, combine rice and 3 tablespoons water. Cover. Heat in the microwave for 3 minutes or until rice is tender. Fluff with a fork.
2. Beat egg with a whisk or fork. In a medium bowl, combine ground beef, egg, cooked rice, onion powder, oregano, Worcestershire sauce, and ⅛ teaspoon black pepper. Mix.
3. Divide meatball mixture into 12 even portions (1 ounce each). Roll into meatballs. Place meatballs on a baking sheet. Bake for 10 minutes. Heat to an internal temperature of 165° F.
4. In a small microwave-safe bowl, heat marinara sauce in the microwave for 2 minutes. Stir. Serve 2 meatballs with ¼ cup sauce.

Yield: 6 servings
Meal Component: Meat/Meat Alternate, Vegetable

Serving sizes are for ages 3–5. Guidelines for the proper credit of food may vary in some states. Please check with the CACFP in your state for more information.

Menu of the Month

Breakfast
Milk
Fruit and Yogurt Roll-Ups*
(WG)

Morning Snack
Water
Whole Grain Pretzels (WG)
Raspberries

Lunch
Milk
Meatballs and Marinara*
Whole Wheat Penne Pasta
(WG)
Canned Pears

Afternoon Snack
Water
Celery
Sunflower Butter

*Indicates recipes of the month.
(WG) Indicates whole grain
Recipes adapted from the Institute of Childhood Nutrition.

Nutrition and Fitness Notes

Facilitate physical development, motor coordination, and fitness by supporting children when they run, jump, balance, throw balls, dance to music, and participate in other noncompetitive movement activities. Encourage all children to try a variety of activities and to develop skill and enjoyment in moving their bodies. Promote movement, activity, and fun—not competitiveness.

The Experienced Provider

While rare, injuries and deaths do occur in child care. Because of this, it's important to be as proactive as possible when examining your environment. We know most young children fall frequently as they're learning to stand and walk. Create environments that acknowledge how young children develop while continuing to keep them safe. Restraining young children in a manner that impedes their development is not a legitimate safety plan.

Activities for Children

Bounces and Collisions
Show children objects and have them guess which ones will bounce. Let them try to balance the objects on their feet, stomachs, hands, and heads while lying down and standing up. When objects fall off, help children measure how high they bounce. Introduce the word *collision* and explain that a collision occurs when something bounces. As follow-up, look for and discuss other collisions.

Child-Designed Inclines
This activity allows children to experiment with the effects of changing the slope and direction of inclined planes. Provide a flannel or magnetic board, mounted to the wall or propped vertically; four to eight small ramps; and small balls. Construct the ramps by removing the ends from small cardboard jewelry gift boxes, approximately 8 inches long and 2 inches wide, and affix either Velcro or magnetic tape to the long edges. Children can change the angle, position, and direction of each ramp segment and observe how the change affects the movement of the balls.

Sports Dreams
Books in which children stand up to limiting gender norms, including books that portray girls engaging in athletic activities, show children that they can follow their passions and interests regardless of their gender. Read *Allie's Basketball Dream* by Barbara Barber and then let children play basketball with child-size goals or by using soft balls and hula hoops.

Literacy Corner

I Got Next by Daria Peoples-Riley
In this action-packed picture book, a young basketball player gets ready for a neighborhood pickup game.

The Bat Boy and His Violin by Gavin Curtis
A young aspiring violinist learns the value of family ties and team spirit in this picture book about a down-on-their-luck baseball team.

JULY ATTENDANCE AND PAYMENT LOG

To record drop-off and pickup times that vary, try using two lines per child.

CHILD'S NAME	S	M 1	T 2	W 3	T 4	F 5	S	TOTAL	S 6	M 7	T 8	W 9	T 10	F 11	S 12	TOTAL	S 13	M 14	T 15	W 16	T 17	F 18	S 19	TOTAL	S 20	M 21	T 22	W 23	T 24	F 25	S 26	TOTAL	S 27	M 28	T 29	W 30	T 31	F	S	TOTAL	S	M

JULY ATTENDANCE AND PAYMENT LOG CONTINUED

CHILD'S NAME	S	M T W T F S	TOTAL	S M T W T F S	TOTAL	S M T W T F S	TOTAL	S M T W T F S	TOTAL	S M T W T F S	TOTAL	S M
		1 2 3 4 5		6 7 8 9 10 11 12		13 14 15 16 17 18 19		20 21 22 23 24 25 26		27 28 29 30 31		

WEEKLY PAYMENT TOTALS

	FOOD PROGRAM INCOME RECVD	PARENT FEE INCOME RECVD	OTHER INCOME RECVD			
JULY INCOME				=	JUL TOTAL	
BALANCE FORWARD				=	BALANCE FWD TOTAL	
TOTAL Y-T-D INCOME				=	TOTAL Y-T-D	

Food Program Claim

Date Claim Sent _____

Date Check Received _____

MEAL COUNT TALLY

BREAKFASTS	
LUNCHES	
DINNERS	
SNACKS	

Put totals in year-end meal tally, page 95.

JULY EXPENSE REPORT

DATE	PAYMENT TYPE cash, check #, cc #, debit	PURCHASED FROM	PURCHASE TOTAL	ADVERTISING	INSURANCE	INTEREST	LEGAL & PROFESSIONAL SERVICES	OFFICE EXPENSES (including internet & 2nd phone)	RENT OF BUSINESS PROPERTY	REPAIR & MAINTENANCE	SUPPLIES		MILES
		THIS MONTH'S TOTAL											
		BALANCE CARRIED FORWARD											
		YEAR-TO-DATE TOTAL											

JULY EXPENSE REPORT

DATE	PAYMENT TYPE cash, check #, cc #, debit	PURCHASED FROM	PURCHASE TOTAL	TAXES & LICENSES	TRAVEL & ENTERTAINMENT	FOOD	TOYS	HOUSEHOLD ITEMS	CLEANING SUPPLIES	ACTIVITY EXPENSES			MILES
		THIS MONTH'S TOTAL											
		BALANCE CARRIED FORWARD											
		YEAR-TO-DATE TOTAL											

See page 85 for an explanation of how to transfer expenses to your tax forms. You may wish to relabel the columns to fit your business needs.

See page 6 for an explanation of the order in which we present the categories.

AUGUST 2025

Hours Worked
- Previous Total
- No. Hours Open*
- Other Hours Worked**
- Year-to-Date Total

* "No. Hours Open" refers to hours from when the first child arrived to when the last child left (not your advertised work hours).
** "Other Hours Worked" refers to hours spent on business activities in the home (cleaning, meal preparation, activity planning, and so on) when children are not present.

SUN	MON	TUE	WED	THU	FRI	SAT
JULY 2025	SEPTEMBER 2025				1	2
3 Tishah B'Av (Jewish)	4 Fire Drill Day	5	6	7	8	9
10	11	12	13 Severe Storm Drill Day	14	15	16
17	18	19	20	21	22	23
24 / 31	25	26 Women's Equality Day	27	28	29 Call your local R & R agency; update your service	30

AUGUST

Nature and Me
Being outside is such fun—
Birds, leaves, insects, laughter, sun!

Recipes

Egg and Broccoli Scramble

6 eggs
½ teaspoon garlic powder
1 tablespoon Parmesan cheese
5 ounces frozen broccoli, thawed, drained, and chopped

1. In a medium bowl, combine eggs, 1 tablespoon water, garlic powder, Parmesan cheese, and salt and pepper to taste. Whisk to mix.
2. Spray a small nonstick skillet with nonstick cooking spray. Heat skillet on medium-high heat. Sauté thawed broccoli for 3–5 minutes or until broccoli begins to turn brown on the tips of the crowns.
3. Add egg mixture. Stir eggs and broccoli, constantly removing any egg sticking to the bottom of the pan, until eggs reach 160° F.

Yield: 6 servings, ⅓ cup each
Meal Component: Meat/Meat Alternate

Caprese Bruschetta

3 cups diced fresh tomatoes
½ teaspoon minced fresh garlic
2 tablespoons chopped fresh basil
1 tablespoon balsamic vinegar
1 teaspoon olive oil
¼ teaspoon salt
¼ cup shredded part-skim mozzarella
3 whole wheat sandwich thins, at least 2 ounces each

1. Preheat oven to 350° F. In a medium bowl, stir together tomatoes, garlic, basil, balsamic vinegar, olive oil, salt, and mozzarella cheese.
2. Separate sandwich thins and place both halves on a baking sheet. Bake for about 6–8 minutes or until toasted.
3. Place ½ cup tomato mixture on each toasted half..

Yield: 6 servings
Meal Component: Grain, Vegetable

Menu of the Month

Breakfast
Milk
Egg and Broccoli Scramble*
Peaches

Morning Snack
Water
Mini Whole Grain Waffles (WG)
Mashed Strawberries

Lunch
Milk
Bean and Cheese Burritos
Watermelon
Vegetable Kebobs

Afternoon Snack
Water
Caprese Bruschetta* (WG)

*Indicates recipes of the month.
(WG) Indicates whole grain
Recipes adapted from the Institute of Childhood Nutrition.

Nutrition and Fitness Notes

Prepare food for children just before meal- or snacktime, and serve the food immediately. Leftovers should not remain at room temperature for more than 30 minutes and should be covered and stored in a refrigerator. Contact the local health department for information on cleaning food utensils and proper food preparation and storage.

The Experienced Provider

Time spent in scientific investigations outdoors helps children understand the ebb and flow of life around them. Children can observe and investigate plant growth. They may pick dandelions and notice the parts of the plant. They might observe differences between moss and grass. Where there is no space to garden in the ground, children can create container gardens. They can also watch neighborhood animals, such as birds, squirrels, and insects, and find ways to interact with them, such as by filling a bird feeder or observing what foods ants like to eat.

Activities for Children

Nature's Shapes
Provide materials for children to identify geometric shapes found in nature and to group objects based on this attribute. Some ideas: Circular or spherical—a small bird's nest, a buckeye, a sweet gum pod; oval or ovoid—a cowrie seashell, a pumpkin seed, a leaf from a jade plant; triangular or conical—a fern (preserved in self-laminating film), a pinecone, a feather; pentagon—a dried apple slice showing the core, a flower (preserved in self-laminating film), a starfish; hexagon—a wasp comb, a large leaf, a flower. Also provide plastic containers with shape signs showing geometric shapes, for sorting, as well as photographs of geometric shapes in nature and books on the topic.

Tracing Shadows
Pick a sunny day when it is not too close to noon. Children work in pairs, or the educator can assist. While one child stands still, another child uses sidewalk chalk to trace their partner's shadow. Write children's names inside the shadow outlines so they can return later and compare their current shadow to the shadow outline. Measurement terms such as *little*, *big*, *longer*, and *shorter* can be used during these observations. Older children can use interlocking cubes, such as Unifix, or a standard measuring tool to compare lengths.

Different Perspectives
Educators should intentionally highlight differences in opinions and experiences so children become aware of social differences and so all children feel they belong in the classroom. One way to do this is to ask for different perspectives on situations instead of assuming that all children are excited or sad about the same things.

Literacy Corner

Bree Finds a Friend by Mike Huber
Bree is digging for worms, but she unearths something even better than she expected—a new friend!

nipêhon / I Wait by Caitlin Dale Nicholson
A young child, her grandmother, and mother are going out to pick wild yarrow in this quiet, gentle story about a family working together written in Cree and English.

AUGUST ATTENDANCE AND PAYMENT LOG

To record drop-off and pickup times that vary, try using two lines per child.

CHILD'S NAME	S	M	T	W	T	F 1	S 2	TOTAL	S 3	M 4	T 5	W 6	T 7	F 8	S 9	TOTAL	S 10	M 11	T 12	W 13	T 14	F 15	S 16	TOTAL	S 17	M 18	T 19	W 20	T 21	F 22	S 23	TOTAL	S 24	M 25	T 26	W 27	T 28	F 29	S 30	TOTAL	S 31	M

AUGUST ATTENDANCE AND PAYMENT LOG CONTINUED

CHILD'S NAME	S	M	T	W	T	F 1	S 2	TOTAL	S 3	M 4	T 5	W 6	T 7	F 8	S 9	TOTAL	S 10	M 11	T 12	W 13	T 14	F 15	S 16	TOTAL	S 17	M 18	T 19	W 20	T 21	F 22	S 23	TOTAL	S 24	M 25	T 26	W 27	T 28	F 29	S 30	TOTAL	S 31	M

WEEKLY PAYMENT TOTALS

	FOOD PROGRAM INCOME RECVD	PARENT FEE INCOME RECVD	OTHER INCOME RECVD			
AUGUST INCOME				=	AUG TOTAL	
BALANCE FORWARD				=	BALANCE FWD TOTAL	
TOTAL Y-T-D INCOME				=	TOTAL Y-T-D	

Food Program Claim

Date Claim Sent _____

Date Check Received _____

MEAL COUNT TALLY

BREAKFASTS	
LUNCHES	
DINNERS	
SNACKS	

Put totals in year-end meal tally, page 95.

AUGUST EXPENSE REPORT

DATE	PAYMENT TYPE cash, check #, cc #, debit	PURCHASED FROM	PURCHASE TOTAL	ADVERTISING	INSURANCE	INTEREST	LEGAL & PROFESSIONAL SERVICES	OFFICE EXPENSES (including internet & 2nd phone)	RENT OF BUSINESS PROPERTY	REPAIR & MAINTENANCE	SUPPLIES		MILES
		THIS MONTH'S TOTAL											
		BALANCE CARRIED FORWARD											
		YEAR-TO-DATE TOTAL											

AUGUST EXPENSE REPORT

DATE	PAYMENT TYPE cash, check #, cc #, debit	PURCHASED FROM	PURCHASE TOTAL	TAXES & LICENSES	TRAVEL & ENTERTAINMENT	FOOD	TOYS	HOUSEHOLD ITEMS	CLEANING SUPPLIES	ACTIVITY EXPENSES			MILES
			THIS MONTH'S TOTAL										
			BALANCE CARRIED FORWARD										
			YEAR-TO-DATE TOTAL										

See page 85 for an explanation of how to transfer expenses to your tax forms. You may wish to relabel the columns to fit your business needs.

See page 6 for an explanation of the order in which we present the categories.

SEPTEMBER 2025

Hours Worked	
Previous Total	
No. Hours Open*	
Other Hours Worked**	
Year-to-Date Total	

* "No. Hours Open" refers to hours from when the first child arrived to when the last child left (not your advertised work hours).
** "Other Hours Worked" refers to hours spent on business activities in the home (cleaning, meal preparation, activity planning, and so on) when children are not present.

SUN	MON	TUE	WED	THU	FRI	SAT
	1 Labor Day	2	3	4	5 Mawlid al-Nabi (Islamic)	6
7 Grandparents' Day	8 Fire Drill Day	9	10 Severe Storm Drill Day	11 Patriot Day	12	13
14	15 Start of National Hispanic Heritage Month 2025 3rd quarter estimated taxes due	16	17 Constitution Day	18	19	20
21	22 Autumn begins Change your smoke alarm and carbon monoxide filter batteries	23 Rosh Hashanah (Jewish)	24	25	26 Native American Day	27
28	29	30 Call your local R & R agency; update your service				

The Redleaf Calendar-Keeper™ 2026 is available now!

AUGUST 2025
S	M	T	W	T	F	S
					1	2
3	4	5	6	7	8	9
10	11	12	13	14	15	16
17	18	19	20	21	22	23
24	25	26	27	28	29	30
31						

OCTOBER 2025
S	M	T	W	T	F	S
			1	2	3	4
5	6	7	8	9	10	11
12	13	14	15	16	17	18
19	20	21	22	23	24	25
26	27	28	29	30	31	

SEPTEMBER

Playing Together
We have so much fun with friends,
We hope this day never ends!

Recipes

Oven-Baked Pancakes with Spiced Pears

½ cup whole wheat pancake mix
2 15-ounce cans pears in extra-light syrup, syrup reserved
1 tablespoon cornstarch
1 teaspoon pumpkin pie spice
½ teaspoon vanilla extract

1. Preheat oven to 375° F. Grease a loaf pan. In a bowl, combine pancake mix and ½ cup water. Whisk until smooth. Pour pancake batter into loaf pan and bake for 35 minutes.
2. Separate pears and syrup, reserving syrup. Dice pears and place in a small bowl.
3. Pour syrup into a medium nonstick pot. Add cornstarch, pumpkin pie spice, and vanilla extract to syrup. Whisk until smooth. Heat syrup mixture on medium-high heat and whisk continuously until it begins to boil, about 5 minutes.
4. Add pears to syrup mixture. Stir. Bring mixture to a boil, about 7 minutes. Reduce heat and simmer for 3–5 minutes or until it becomes nectar-thick. Stir often to prevent sticking.
5. Slice pancake into 6 pieces and serve with pears.

Yield: 6 servings, 1 pancake slice and ½ cup pears each
Meal Component: Grain, Fruit

Baked Tilapia Fillets

¼ cup whole wheat seasoned breadcrumbs
½ teaspoon Herbs de Provence seasoning blend
13½ ounces tilapia fillets (fresh or frozen, thawed)
4 teaspoons reduced-fat mayonnaise

1. Preheat oven to 400° F. Place a baking rack on top of a baking sheet and spray with nonstick cooking spray.
2. In a small bowl, combine breadcrumbs and Herbs de Provence.
3. Lightly coat each piece of fish with mayonnaise. Top coated fish with the seasoned breadcrumb mixture. Place on prepared baking rack. Bake for 15 minutes, to an internal temperature of 145° F. Flesh should be opaque and separate easily with a fork.

Yield: 6 servings, one fillet each
Meal Component: Meat/Meat Alternate

Menu of the Month

Breakfast
Milk
Oven-Baked Pancakes with Spiced Pears* (WG)

Morning Snack
Water
Whole Grain Crackers
Cheese Cubes

Lunch
Milk
Baked Tilapia Fillets*
Whole Wheat Bread Stick (WG)
Steamed Brussels Sprouts
Mixed Fruit Salad

Afternoon Snack
Water
Peas in the Pod
Plain Popcorn

*Indicates recipes of the month.
(WG) Indicates whole grain
Recipes adapted from the Institute of Childhood Nutrition.

Nutrition and Fitness Notes

Be prepared to address issues regarding food sharing: whether children are allowed to bring food from home and, if so, what measures are in place to ensure proper nutrition and to meet additional storage requirements; whether children are allowed to share food with other children; and what policies need to be set for food adults provide for the program on special occasions.

The Experienced Provider

Be a keen observer of children's play, conversations, and activity to identify their interests. Watch for children's attentiveness, persistence, and total absorption. Observe their facial expressions and actions. Take note of their words. Search for insights that will guide you in discovering children's emerging capabilities and captivations. Close observation reveals each child's distinctive qualities, passions, and interests and directs educators in how to support and extend their fascinations.

Activities for Children

The Joy of Play
Playing group games embodies our collective joy! Playing games together provides a great opportunity for children to practice their natural social skills and grow their relationships. This play often generates something new and never before thought of while also carrying the traditions and ideas from one generation to the next—like the legacy of hopscotch. What games do you remember playing as a child? In what ways do you share games from your childhood with the children you work with? What shared games do you still love to play?

Loose Parts and Social Skills
Social skills such as sharing, contributing, leading, and following develop as children share space and loose parts, showing consideration for and cooperation with others. Play in a construction zone, for example, offers social opportunities for children to cooperate, communicate, and problem solve as they build. When collaborating on building a structure such as a skyscraper, children must negotiate and work through problems and disagreements that arise.

Discussing Conflict
One culturally responsive approach for supporting healthy social-emotional development and dealing with challenging behaviors is to discuss conflict during group time. This approach is a great way to tackle harmful racial comments made by children. By discussing those situations in a group, all children can learn why certain comments are harmful and how they make their peers feel, which could prevent additional future harm.

Literacy Corner

My Three Best Friends & Me, Zulay by Cari Best
With the support of her friends, Zulay, who is blind, gets ready to run a race.

The Homesick Club by Libby Martinez
Schoolkids Mónica and Hannah form the Homesick Club, since they are both from far away, and soon they invite their new teacher to join.

Serving sizes are for ages 3–5. Guidelines for the proper credit of food may vary in some states. Please check with the CACFP in your state for more information.

SEPTEMBER ATTENDANCE AND PAYMENT LOG

To record drop-off and pickup times that vary, try using two lines per child.

CHILD'S NAME	S 1	M 2	T 3	W 4	T 5	F 6	S	TOTAL	S 7	M 8	T 9	W 10	T 11	F 12	S 13	TOTAL	S 14	M 15	T 16	W 17	T 18	F 19	S 20	TOTAL	S 21	M 22	T 23	W 24	T 25	F 26	S 27	TOTAL	S 28	M 29	T 30	W	T	F	S	TOTAL	S	M

SEPTEMBER ATTENDANCE AND PAYMENT LOG CONTINUED

CHILD'S NAME	S 1	M 2	T 3	W 4	T 5	F 6	S	TOTAL	S 7	M 8	T 9	W 10	T 11	F 12	S 13	TOTAL	S 14	M 15	T 16	W 17	T 18	F 19	S 20	TOTAL	S 21	M 22	T 23	W 24	T 25	F 26	S 27	TOTAL	S 28	M 29	T 30	W	T	F	S	TOTAL	S	M

WEEKLY PAYMENT TOTALS

	FOOD PROGRAM INCOME RECVD	PARENT FEE INCOME RECVD	OTHER INCOME RECVD			
SEPTEMBER INCOME				=	SEPT TOTAL	
BALANCE FORWARD				=	BALANCE FWD TOTAL	
TOTAL Y-T-D INCOME				=	TOTAL Y-T-D	

Food Program Claim

Date Claim Sent _____

Date Check Received _____

MEAL COUNT TALLY

BREAKFASTS	
LUNCHES	
DINNERS	
SNACKS	

Put totals in year-end meal tally, page 95.

SEPTEMBER EXPENSE REPORT

DATE	PAYMENT TYPE cash, check #, cc #, debit	PURCHASED FROM	PURCHASE TOTAL	ADVERTISING	INSURANCE	INTEREST	LEGAL & PROFESSIONAL SERVICES	OFFICE EXPENSES (including internet & 2nd phone)	RENT OF BUSINESS PROPERTY	REPAIR & MAINTENANCE	SUPPLIES		MILES
		THIS MONTH'S TOTAL											
		BALANCE CARRIED FORWARD											
		YEAR-TO-DATE TOTAL											

SEPTEMBER EXPENSE REPORT

DATE	PAYMENT TYPE cash, check #, cc #, debit	PURCHASED FROM	PURCHASE TOTAL	TAXES & LICENSES	TRAVEL & ENTERTAINMENT	FOOD	TOYS	HOUSEHOLD ITEMS	CLEANING SUPPLIES	ACTIVITY EXPENSES			MILES
		THIS MONTH'S TOTAL											
		BALANCE CARRIED FORWARD											
		YEAR-TO-DATE TOTAL											

See page 85 for an explanation of how to transfer expenses to your tax forms.
You may wish to relabel the columns to fit your business needs.

See page 6 for an explanation of the order in which we present the categories.

OCTOBER 2025

	Hours Worked
Previous Total	
No. Hours Open*	
Other Hours Worked**	
Year-to-Date Total	

* "No. Hours Open" refers to hours from when the first child arrived to when the last child left (not your advertised work hours).
** "Other Hours Worked" refers to hours spent on business activities in the home (cleaning, meal preparation, activity planning, and so on) when children are not present.

SUN	MON	TUE	WED	THU	FRI	SAT
SEPTEMBER 2025 / NOVEMBER 2025			**1** National Bullying Prevention Month; Breast Cancer Awareness Month	**2** Yom Kippur (Jewish)	**3**	**4**
5	**6** Child Health Day; Fire Drill Day	**7** Sukkot begins (Jewish)	**8** Severe Storm Drill Day	**9**	**10**	**11**
12	**13** Columbus Day; Indigenous Peoples' Day; Sukkot ends (Jewish)	**14**	**15** End of National Hispanic Heritage Month	**16**	**17**	**18**
19	**20** Diwalli (Hindu)	**21**	**22**	**23**	**24**	**25**
26	**27**	**28**	**29**	**30** Call your local R & R agency; update your service	**31** Halloween	

Time Flies
When You're Running a Business!

Now is the perfect time to place your order for the business essentials you'll need next year. Order now and you'll be ready to go for 2026.

The Redleaf Calendar-Keeper™ 2026
A Record-Keeping System for Family Child Care Professionals

Year after year, *The Redleaf Calendar-Keeper* is the most reliable organizational resource for family child care professionals. Continue to save time and money by ordering your 2026 edition now!

#100026-CK25 $21.95

Family Child Care Business Receipt Book

Improve your record keeping with receipts designed specifically for family child care. Three books, each with 50 carbonless duplicate sets of receipts, are included.

#106101-CK25 $15.95

Family Child Care Mileage-Keeper

Record business trips, repairs, tolls, parking, and other car expenses. Forms are included for one year's worth of records.

#104101-CK25 $7.95

Family Child Care Inventory-Keeper

Track furniture, appliances, and other property used in your business for depreciation and insurance purposes.

#107001-CK25 $14.95

Family Child Care Sharing in the Caring
Agreement Packet for Parents and Providers

Establish a clear understanding with parents from the start. This packet contains five copies of a formal two-part agreement form as well as instructions for how to complete contract terms for rates, holidays, vacations, payment dates, and illnesses.

#101301-CK25 $9.95
Forms only (pack of five) #101601-CK25 $8.95

See pages 5 and 66 for additional resources.

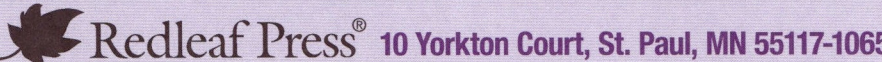

Call 800-423-8309 • Fax 800-641-0115 • www.redleafpress.org

Name _____

Address _____ Apt. ____

City _____

State ____ Zip Code _____-____   **24CK**

Daytime phone (____) _____ E-mail _____

QTY	ITEM #	TITLE	CATALOG PRICE	AMOUNT

Shipping & Handling Charges

Order Size.........Add
$0 to $49.99.........$7.95
$50.00 to $99.99.....$10.95
$100.00 to $149.99...$13.95
$150.00 or more......10% of net order

SUBTOTAL
Shipping/Handling
Your applicable state* and county sales TAX
TOTAL

Alaska, Hawaii, and APO orders are shipped by priority mail; standard rates apply. Foreign orders are shipped by U.S. Postal Service. Call for pricing.

*We currently collect sales tax in these states: IL, IN, KS, MA, MD, MI, MN, NC, NY, OK, PA, TN, VA, WI.

Payment: (U.S. funds only. Sorry, we cannot accept COD orders.)

☐ Check or money order enclosed. DO NOT send cash.

Charge to credit card: ☐ Visa ☐ MC ☐ Discover ☐ American Express

☐☐☐☐ ☐☐☐☐ ☐☐☐☐ ☐☐☐☐   Expiration Date ☐☐ ☐☐
                                              Month Year

☐☐☐ CVN (3-digit code on the back of card)

Cardholder signature (required) _____

Prices subject to change without notice.

Tom Copeland Resources

Tom Copeland, JD, is a licensed attorney, leading tax specialist, and award-winning advocate for the business of family child care.

NEW! Family Child Care 2024 Tax Workbook and Organizer
Tom Copeland is the nation's leading expert on the business of family child care. Updated annually, this is the most comprehensive resource available. This edition contains guidance on navigating new tax laws, tips to help save money, and tools that take the guesswork out of family child care business taxes. Softbound, 264 pgs.

#100824-CK25 $21.95

NEW! Family Child Care 2024 Tax Companion
The *Tax Companion* is a comprehensive tool that will help tax preparers understand the rules that affect family child care businesses. It also includes information on the new tax laws that relate to depreciation. Using this resource will increase your confidence in the tax professionals who prepare your return, help you identify potential errors before your taxes are filed, and ensure that your tax preparer is claiming all allowable deductions. Softbound, 80 pgs.

#101024-CK25 $21.95

The Business of Family Child Care: Contacts and Policies
Most family child care providers would rather care for children than write and enforce contracts and policies, but taking care of the children is only part of the job. Contracts and policies are another important part of running a business. This video can help you understand how to establish a good business relationship with the families you serve by creating clear contracts and policies and enforcing them fairly.

#548029-CK25 $49.95

The Business of Family Child Care: Record-Keeping
Most family child care providers would rather care for children than spend time keeping records. But record keeping is an important part of running a business. This training video can help you understand proper record-keeping strategies, help lower taxes, and save family child care providers money.

#547329-CK25 $79.95

Family Child Care Record-Keeping Guide, 9th Edition
Keep your business organized with the latest information and advice to help you maintain important records. This edition includes descriptions of new depreciation rules, clarifications on deductions, updated resource links, and much more. Softbound, 216 pgs.

#543970-CK25 $21.95

Family Child Care Contracts and Policies, 4th Edition
This edition of the family child care classic offers expanded information on handling rates, late payments, and other fees in your contract; resolving disputes with clients; writing comprehensive policies; and enforcing and terminating your contract. Softbound, 184 pgs.

#546506-CK25 $21.95

Family Child Care Marketing Guide, 2nd Edition
Maximize your enrollment and find inexpensive ways to promote your business. Dozens of marketing tips, information on setting rates, and guidance for using electronic media are included. Softbound, 216 pgs.

#541129-CK25 $18.95

Family Child Care Legal and Insurance Guide
From purchasing insurance to incorporating your business, this indispensable guide details the ways you can reduce the risks and ensure the health and prosperity of your business. Softbound, 224 pgs.

#108501-CK25 $21.95

Family Child Care Business Planning Guide
Whether you are just starting out or have an established operation, a business plan is an essential tool for success. Find information on how to write and use your plan to effectively manage your business. Softbound, 96 pgs.

#112901-CK25 $21.95

Family Child Care Money Management and Retirement Guide
Find valuable information for your business, including how to earn more money and reduce your expenses, plan for retirement, and handle special financial situations. Softbound, 208 pgs.

#112801-CK25 $18.95

OCTOBER

Fun with Math
Measure, tally, count, and add—
Learning math makes us so glad!

Recipes

Breakfast Black Beans with Eggs
2 large eggs
3¾ cups canned black beans, drained (about 2½ 15-ounce cans)
¾ cup canned petite diced tomatoes with onions and garlic in juice
1 teaspoon ground cumin
½ teaspoon salt
¼ cup fresh chopped cilantro

1. Boil eggs: Place eggs in a large pot. Add water until there is 1 inch of water above eggs. Place on stove on medium-high heat. Bring to a boil, and then remove eggs from heat. Cover and let eggs stand in hot water for 12 minutes to hard-boil eggs.
2. While eggs are cooking, place ice and water in a large bowl. When eggs are cooked, remove eggs from hot water with a slotted spoon. Place in the ice bath for 10 minutes.
3. Prepare bean mixture: Heat a medium nonstick skillet on medium-high heat. Spray with nonstick cooking spray. Add beans, tomatoes with juice, ¼ cup water, cumin, and salt. Stir. Bring to a boil and reduce heat to medium. Simmer for 5 minutes.
4. Peel and cut each egg into 3 pieces. Serve ½ cup bean mixture, ⅓ of an egg (1 piece), and chopped cilantro.

Yield: 6 servings
Meal Component: Meat/Meat Alternate, Vegetable

Ginger Carrots
2 cups fresh, diagonally sliced carrots
1 tablespoon honey
1 teaspoon lemon juice
1 teaspoon dried parsley (optional)
1 teaspoon trans-fat-free margarine
½ teaspoon fresh grated ginger

Serving sizes are for ages 3–5. Guidelines for the proper credit of food may vary in some states. Please check with the CACFP in your state for more information.

Menu of the Month

Breakfast
Milk
Breakfast Black Beans with Eggs*

Morning Snack
Water
Almonds
Clementines

Lunch
Milk
Sloppy Joes on Whole Wheat Buns (WG)
Ginger Carrots*
Applesauce

Afternoon Snack
100% Orange Juice
Whole Grain-Rich Puffed Cereal

*Indicates recipes of the month.
(WG) Indicates whole grain
Recipes adapted from the Institute of Childhood Nutrition.

1. Add 1–2 inches of water to a small stockpot with a steamer basket or a double boiler. Bring water to a rolling boil. Add carrots to the steamer basket or double boiler, and cook until carrots are tender but not mushy, 9–10 minutes.
2. Prepare ginger glaze while carrots are cooking by combining the remaining ingredients in a medium mixing bowl. Pour hot steamed carrots into the ginger glaze, and stir until honey and margarine melt.

Yield: 6 servings, ¼ cup each
Meal Component: Vegetable

Nutrition and Fitness Notes

Offer nutritious, appetizing choices of food, and help children self-serve appropriate portions of each food. Some children may want to take large amounts of favorite foods. They may be more comfortable taking small portions if they know they can have second servings when they still feel hungry. Serve all foods at one time, and allow children to eat foods in the order they prefer.

The Experienced Provider

Science and mathematics are embedded in all areas of the learning environment. Cooking experiences introduce children to simple machines through a variety of tools and gadgets. Children discover changes in materials caused by heat, cold, or combination with other materials. Children also use measurement and quantification as they add ingredients.

Activities for Children

Loose Parts Math
Young children naturally construct math concepts while playing with loose parts. Acorns, seashells, pinecones, and sea glass encourage patterning, ordering, comparing, contrasting, classifying, counting, and measuring. Using loose parts, children develop other math concepts, such as symmetry, shape, size, number, space, geometry, fractions, and part/whole relationships. Loose parts are a key element of authentic mathematical learning in early childhood.

Measuring Pumpkins
Provide a small, medium, and large pumpkin plus a measuring tool such as interconnecting plastic links. Invite children to measure the pumpkins in several ways. 1) *Height and circumference*. Children can compare by looking, or measure them. Children's measurements will likely vary; encourage conversations about these discrepancies. 2) *Area*. Children can understand the concept of area by tracing around the bottom of each pumpkin, cutting out the shapes, and laying them on top of one another. 3) *Mass/weight*. The larger pumpkins are too big to measure on a typical school balance scale, but they can be measured on a teeter-totter, balancing against uniform wooden blocks.

Diversity in Groups
Help children understand there is as much diversity within racial groups as across them. There are plenty of things to have in common with other people. Support children's developing racial identities by reading books that authentically portray their lived experiences.

Literacy Corner

Ten, Nine, Eight by Molly Bang
This award-winning classic shares the going-to-bed countdown in a loving family.

Round Is a Mooncake: A Book of Shapes by Roseanne Thong
A little girl's urban neighborhood becomes a discovery ground for shapes in this lyrical picture book.

Call 800-423-8309 to order or shop online at RedleafPress.org

OCTOBER ATTENDANCE AND PAYMENT LOG

To record drop-off and pickup times that vary, try using two lines per child.

CHILD'S NAME	S	M	T 1	W 2	T 3	F 4	S	TOTAL	S 5	M 6	T 7	W 8	T 9	F 10	S 11	TOTAL	S 12	M 13	T 14	W 15	T 16	F 17	S 18	TOTAL	S 19	M 20	T 21	W 22	T 23	F 24	S 25	TOTAL	S 26	M 27	T 28	W 29	T 30	F 31	S	TOTAL	S	M

OCTOBER ATTENDANCE AND PAYMENT LOG CONTINUED

CHILD'S NAME	S	M	T	W	T	F	S	TOTAL	S	M	T	W	T	F	S	TOTAL	S	M	T	W	T	F	S	TOTAL	S	M	T	W	T	F	S	TOTAL	S	M	T	W	T	F	S	TOTAL	S	M
		1	2	3	4	5	6			5	6	7	8	9	10	11		12	13	14	15	16	17	18		19	20	21	22	23	24	25		26	27	28	29	30	31			

WEEKLY PAYMENT TOTALS

	FOOD PROGRAM INCOME RECVD	PARENT FEE INCOME RECVD	OTHER INCOME RECVD			
OCTOBER INCOME				=	OCT TOTAL	
BALANCE FORWARD				=	BALANCE FWD TOTAL	
TOTAL Y-T-D INCOME				=	TOTAL Y-T-D	

Food Program Claim

Date Claim Sent _____

Date Check Received _____

MEAL COUNT TALLY

BREAKFASTS	
LUNCHES	
DINNERS	
SNACKS	

Put totals in year-end meal tally, page 95.

OCTOBER EXPENSE REPORT

DATE	PAYMENT TYPE cash, check #, cc #, debit	PURCHASED FROM	PURCHASE TOTAL	ADVERTISING	INSURANCE	INTEREST	LEGAL & PROFESSIONAL SERVICES	OFFICE EXPENSES (including internet & 2nd phone)	RENT OF BUSINESS PROPERTY	REPAIR & MAINTENANCE	SUPPLIES		MILES
		THIS MONTH'S TOTAL											
		BALANCE CARRIED FORWARD											
		YEAR-TO-DATE TOTAL											

OCTOBER EXPENSE REPORT

DATE	PAYMENT TYPE cash, check #, cc #, debit	PURCHASED FROM	PURCHASE TOTAL	TAXES & LICENSES	TRAVEL & ENTERTAINMENT	FOOD	TOYS	HOUSEHOLD ITEMS	CLEANING SUPPLIES	ACTIVITY EXPENSES			MILES
		THIS MONTH'S TOTAL											
		BALANCE CARRIED FORWARD											
		YEAR-TO-DATE TOTAL											

See page 85 for an explanation of how to transfer expenses to your tax forms. You may wish to relabel the columns to fit your business needs.

See page 6 for an explanation of the order in which we present the categories.

NOVEMBER 2025

Hours Worked	
Previous Total	
No. Hours Open*	
Other Hours Worked**	
Year-to-Date Total	

* "No. Hours Open" refers to hours from when the first child arrived to when the last child left (not your advertised work hours).
** "Other Hours Worked" refers to hours spent on business activities in the home (cleaning, meal preparation, activity planning, and so on) when children are not present.

SUN	MON	TUE	WED	THU	FRI	SAT
						1 American Indian Heritage Month; All Saints' Day (Catholic)
2 Día de los Muertos; All Souls' Day (Catholic)	**3** Fire Drill Day	**4** Election Day	**5**	**6**	**7**	**8**
9	**10**	**11** Veterans Day	**12** Severe Storm Drill Day	**13**	**14**	**15**
16	**17**	**18**	**19**	**20** Universal Children's Day	**21**	**22**
23	**24**	**25**	**26** Call your local R & R agency; update your service	**27** Thanksgiving Day	**28**	**29**
30 First Sunday of Advent (Christian)						

Be ready for 2026. Order your Redleaf Calendar-Keeper™ 2026 today.

NOVEMBER

Loose Parts for Everyone

Loose parts are for everyone—
Collect them all! It's so much fun!

Recipes

Turkey Sausage with Cran-Apple Topping

4½ ounces 93% lean ground turkey
Seasonings: ¼ teaspoon each ground sage, onion powder, and salt; ⅛ teaspoon pepper
1 cup peeled and diced apples
6 tablespoons dried cranberries
3 tablespoons maple syrup

1. Preheat oven to 400° F. In a small bowl, combine turkey and seasonings. Divide mixture into 6 even portions. Make patties.
2. Place on a baking sheet sprayed with nonstick cooking spray. Bake in the oven for 8–10 minutes, to 165° F.
3. Prepare cran-apple topping: Heat a medium nonstick saucepan on medium heat. Add apples and cook to soften, about 5 minutes. Stir frequently. When apples begin to soften, add dried cranberries and maple syrup. Bring to a light boil, about 2 minutes. Serve 1 patty with 3 tablespoons cran-apple topping.

Yield: 6 servings
Meal Component: Meat/Meat Alternate

Peach and Yogurt Smoothies

7½ cups frozen peaches
1½ cups low-fat vanilla yogurt

1. Combine peaches and yogurt in a blender. Mix until smooth.

Yield: 6 servings, ¾ cup each
Meal Component: Meat/Meat Alternate, Fruit

Serving sizes are for ages 3–5. Guidelines for the proper credit of food may vary in some states. Please check with the CACFP in your state for more information.

Menu of the Month

Breakfast
Milk
Turkey Sausage with Cran-Apple Topping*
Dragonfruit

Morning Snack
Water
Peach and Yogurt Smoothies*

Lunch
Milk
Whole Wheat Spaghetti with Chicken (WG)
Steamed Mixed Frozen Vegetables
Baked Apples

Afternoon Snack
Water
Whole Grain Muffin (WG)
Mixed Nuts

*Indicates recipes of the month.
(WG) Indicates whole grain
Recipes adapted from the Institute of Childhood Nutrition.

Nutrition and Fitness Notes

Encourage children to raise one leg and balance on the other, then switch legs. Then ask children to hop up and down on the balancing leg. Give children any of the following materials to create an obstacle course: a flat rope to create a curved path; long boards to create a straight path; large building blocks and/or clean tires to form a long, low, raised surface. Have children take turns crawling, walking, and hopping across the surface.

The Experienced Provider

Taking stock of what loose parts you currently have is the first step in gaining an accurate assessment of your physical inventory and will help determine appropriate action for provisioning your program. It will help you know which play zones need loose parts as well as which loose parts to acquire. Involve children in the inventory process, as collecting data is part of scientific inquiry. Keeping a record of your loose parts journey will capture where you started and document how the changes affect children's play.

Activities for Children

Fine-Motor Skills
When children manipulate smaller loose parts, muscular coordination of their fingers and hands improves as they grasp, lift, place, reach, release, pour, and scoop. Pincer grasps are used to pick up buttons or colored stones. Squeezing and gripping muscles improve as children explore felted wool balls. Stacking tiles or smooth stones into towers requires precision, dexterity, and coordination of the hands. Hand-eye coordination develops as a child places small seashells on a work surface for exploring, making designs and patterns, or creating representations.

Engaging with Loose Parts
Children do not need to be taught how to use loose parts. They instinctively know what to do with open-ended materials and are intrinsically motivated by their possibilities. Here are some points to keep in mind to foster children's engagement: 1) Provide long blocks of uninterrupted time. 2) Keep spaces flexible and materials open-ended. 3) Provide large quantities of intriguing loose parts both indoors and out. 4) Let children pursue their own interests. Resist the temptation to direct play. 5) Stay close, watch, and listen with genuine attentiveness. Be fully present. Embrace surprises. Curiosity is contagious!

Supporting All Children
Educators must create and design play ecosystems that support children regardless of their ability, race, ethnicity, socioeconomic status, language, family culture, or history. Educators can use a variety of adaptations to increase the participation of children with diverse abilities in the learning ecosystem.

Literacy Corner

Busy Fingers by C. W. Bowie
The chalk illustrations in this board book depict children learning, squishing, playing, and working with their hands.

Radiant Child: The Story of Young Artist Jean-Michel Basquiat by Javaka Steptoe
The story of Jean-Michel Basquiat shares the powerful message that art doesn't always have to be neat or clean—and definitely not inside the lines—to be beautiful.

NOVEMBER ATTENDANCE AND PAYMENT LOG

To record drop-off and pickup times that vary, try using two lines per child.

CHILD'S NAME	S	M	T	W	T	F	S 1	TOTAL	S 2	M 3	T 4	W 5	T 6	F 7	S 8	TOTAL	S 9	M 10	T 11	W 12	T 13	F 14	S 15	TOTAL	S 16	M 17	T 18	W 19	T 20	F 21	S 22	TOTAL	S 23	M 24	T 25	W 26	T 27	F 28	S 29	TOTAL	S 30	M	

NOVEMBER ATTENDANCE AND PAYMENT LOG CONTINUED

CHILD'S NAME	S	M	T	W	T	F	S 1	TOTAL	S 2	M 3	T 4	W 5	T 6	F 7	S 8	TOTAL	S 9	M 10	T 11	W 12	T 13	F 14	S 15	TOTAL	S 16	M 17	T 18	W 19	T 20	F 21	S 22	TOTAL	S 23	M 24	T 25	W 26	T 27	F 28	S 29	TOTAL	S 30	M

WEEKLY PAYMENT TOTALS

	FOOD PROGRAM INCOME RECVD	PARENT FEE INCOME RECVD	OTHER INCOME RECVD			
NOVEMBER INCOME				=	NOV TOTAL	
BALANCE FORWARD				=	BALANCE FWD TOTAL	
TOTAL Y-T-D INCOME				=	TOTAL Y-T-D	

Food Program Claim

Date Claim Sent _____

Date Check Received _____

MEAL COUNT TALLY

BREAKFASTS	
LUNCHES	
DINNERS	
SNACKS	

Put totals in year-end meal tally, page 95.

NOVEMBER EXPENSE REPORT

DATE	PAYMENT TYPE cash, check #, cc #, debit	PURCHASED FROM	PURCHASE TOTAL	ADVERTISING	INSURANCE	INTEREST	LEGAL & PROFESSIONAL SERVICES	OFFICE EXPENSES (including internet & 2nd phone)	RENT OF BUSINESS PROPERTY	REPAIR & MAINTENANCE	SUPPLIES		MILES
		THIS MONTH'S TOTAL											
		BALANCE CARRIED FORWARD											
		YEAR-TO-DATE TOTAL											

NOVEMBER EXPENSE REPORT

DATE	PAYMENT TYPE cash, check #, cc #, debit	PURCHASED FROM	PURCHASE TOTAL	TAXES & LICENSES	TRAVEL & ENTERTAINMENT	FOOD	TOYS	HOUSEHOLD ITEMS	CLEANING SUPPLIES	ACTIVITY EXPENSES			MILES
			THIS MONTH'S TOTAL										
			BALANCE CARRIED FORWARD										
			YEAR-TO-DATE TOTAL										

See page 85 for an explanation of how to transfer expenses to your tax forms. You may wish to relabel the columns to fit your business needs.

See page 6 for an explanation of the order in which we present the categories.

DECEMBER 2025

	Hours Worked
Previous Total	
No. Hours Open*	
Other Hours Worked**	
Year-to-Date Total	

* "No. Hours Open" refers to hours from when the first child arrived to when the last child left (not your advertised work hours).

** "Other Hours Worked" refers to hours spent on business activities in the home (cleaning, meal preparation, activity planning, and so on) when children are not present.

SUN	MON	TUE	WED	THU	FRI	SAT
	1 Fire Drill Day	**2**	**3**	**4**	**5**	**6**
7	**8**	**9**	**10** Human Rights Day Severe Storm Drill Day	**11**	**12**	**13**
14	**15** Hanukkah begins (Jewish)	**16**	**17**	**18**	**19**	**20**
21 Winter begins	**22** Hanukkah ends (Jewish)	**23**	**24** Christmas Eve (Christian)	**25** Christmas Day (Christian)	**26** Boxing Day Kwanzaa begins	**27**
28	**29**	**30** Call your local R & R agency; update your service	**31** New Year's Eve			

Tax season is just around the corner. Don't forget to order your 2025 tax resources!

NOVEMBER 2025

S	M	T	W	T	F	S
						1
2	3	4	5	6	7	8
9	10	11	12	13	14	15
16	17	18	19	20	21	22
23	24	25	26	27	28	29
30						

JANUARY 2026

S	M	T	W	T	F	S
				1	2	3
4	5	6	7	8	9	10
11	12	13	14	15	16	17
18	19	20	21	22	23	24
25	26	27	28	29	30	31

DECEMBER

Reflecting Back
When I reflect it's food for thought,
I realized I have learned a lot!

Recipes

Spiced Oatmeal
2¼ cups low-fat milk
4 teaspoons trans-fat-free margarine
2 tablespoons agave nectar
¼ teaspoon vanilla extract
Seasonings: ¼ teaspoon each ground cinnamon, ground nutmeg, salt
2½ cups rolled oats

1. Bring milk and 2¼ cups water to a boil.
2. Add margarine, agave, vanilla, and seasonings, stirring constantly.
3. Add oats. Reduce heat to medium. Stir constantly for 5–8 minutes until oatmeal slightly thickens. Serve immediately.

Yield: 6 servings, ¾ cup each
Meal Component: Grain

Chickpeas and Tomatoes
1 teaspoon canola oil
1¼ cups diced onions
2 cloves garlic, minced
½ teaspoon grated fresh ginger
2½ cups cooked or canned garbanzo beans (chickpeas), drained and rinsed
3 cups low-sodium canned tomatoes with juice
½ teaspoon chili powder
1½ teaspoons ground cumin

1. Heat oil in a small stockpot on medium–high heat. Add onions and sauté until soft. Do not brown. Add the garlic and ginger; stir until fragrant.
2. Add the garbanzo beans (chickpeas), tomatoes with juice, ¼ cup water, chili powder, and cumin. Continue cooking on medium–high heat, and bring to a boil. Reduce heat to medium, and simmer uncovered for 10 minutes or until there is only enough liquid to cover the bottom of the pan.

Yield: 6 servings, ½ cup each
Meal Component: Meat/Meat Alternate, Vegetable

Menu of the Month

Breakfast
Milk
Spiced Oatmeal* (WG)
Honeydew Melon "Smiles"

Morning Snack
Water
Whole Grain Tortilla (WG)
Deli Turkey

Lunch
Milk
Chickpeas and Tomatoes*
Whole Wheat Biscuit (WG)
Pineapple

Afternoon Snack
Water
Kohlrabi Chunks
Whole Wheat Raisin Bread (WG)

*Indicates recipes of the month.
(WG) Indicates whole grain
Spiced Oatmeal recipe is adapted from the US Department of Agriculture.
Chickpeas and Tomatoes recipe is adapted from the Institute of Childhood Nutrition.

Nutrition and Fitness Notes

Programs may schedule a rest period or encourage children to rest whenever they need to. Some children go to sleep easily, while others may only rest. Some children may be unable to rest quietly if they already have had adequate rest, if they are excited about other activities, or if they fear the dark or being alone. If a child cannot rest, provide time and space for quiet play.

The Experienced Provider

Reflecting on the work we do with children, on who children are, on what children need, and on the ways that children are making meaning in the world is an essential and indispensable piece of our work as early childhood educators. By engaging in sustained reflection, we become ever more alive to the intricacy and vibrancy of children's worlds and prepare ourselves to be better educators and advocates for these young humans who spend so much time with us in community. One of the central pieces of reflection is documentation. Documenting children's experiences means that we spend time taking a close-up look at what has happened or is happening, thinking about how we can respond both in the moment and beyond.

Activities for Children

Expressing Emotions with Loose Parts
Loose parts foster emotional competencies of perseverance, initiative, independence, and self-regulation as children spend long periods of time doing something that piques their curiosity and is intrinsically motivating. Children also use loose parts to express thoughts and feelings that seem overwhelming or unmanageable.

Increasing Children's Agency
Solicit children's ideas. Raise questions about what children like to do in different play areas or zones (e.g., "What do you like to do in the sand area?" "What do you need to do that?"), or make statements such as "I noticed that you were interested in filling the bucket with hazelnuts."

Talking about Differences
When we adults are uncomfortable with differences and don't talk about them as a normal part of our lives, then when children encounter differences they come to think that "there must be something wrong with me" or "there must be something wrong with them." This discomfort harms Black and Brown children who are marginalized in the larger culture, where they don't see themselves represented and are often portrayed as less important members of the community.

Literacy Corner

The Quiet Book by Deborah Underwood
All quiet is not created equal, and this charming picture book captures many different quiet moments.

All the Colors We Are/Todos los colores de nuestra piel: The Story of How We Get Our Skin Color by Katie Kissinger
This book's colorful photographs and engaging text help children understand why our skin comes in a rainbow of colors.

Serving sizes are for ages 3–5. Guidelines for the proper credit of food may vary in some states. Please check with the CACFP in your state for more information.

DECEMBER ATTENDANCE AND PAYMENT LOG

To record drop-off and pickup times that vary, try using two lines per child.

CHILD'S NAME	S 1	M 2	T 3	W 4	T 5	F 6	S	TOTAL	S 7	M 8	T 9	W 10	T 11	F 12	S 13	TOTAL	S 14	M 15	T 16	W 17	T 18	F 19	S 20	TOTAL	S 21	M 22	T 23	W 24	T 25	F 26	S 27	TOTAL	S 28	M 29	T 30	W 31	T	F	S	TOTAL	S	M

DECEMBER ATTENDANCE AND PAYMENT LOG CONTINUED

CHILD'S NAME	S 1	M 2	T 3	W 4	T 5	F 6	S	TOTAL	S 7	M 8	T 9	W 10	T 11	F 12	S 13	TOTAL	S 14	M 15	T 16	W 17	T 18	F 19	S 20	TOTAL	S 21	M 22	T 23	W 24	T 25	F 26	S 27	TOTAL	S 28	M 29	T 30	W 31	T	F	S	TOTAL	S	M

WEEKLY PAYMENT TOTALS

	FOOD PROGRAM INCOME RECVD	PARENT FEE INCOME RECVD	OTHER INCOME RECVD		
DECEMBER INCOME				=	DEC TOTAL
BALANCE FORWARD				=	BALANCE FWD TOTAL
TOTAL Y-T-D INCOME				=	TOTAL Y-T-D

Food Program Claim

Date Claim Sent _____

Date Check Received _____

MEAL COUNT TALLY

BREAKFASTS	
LUNCHES	
DINNERS	
SNACKS	

Put totals in year-end meal tally, page 95.

DECEMBER EXPENSE REPORT

DATE	PAYMENT TYPE cash, check #, cc #, debit	PURCHASED FROM	PURCHASE TOTAL	ADVERTISING	INSURANCE	INTEREST	LEGAL & PROFESSIONAL SERVICES	OFFICE EXPENSES (including internet & 2nd phone)	RENT OF BUSINESS PROPERTY	REPAIR & MAINTENANCE	SUPPLIES		MILES
		THIS MONTH'S TOTAL											
		BALANCE CARRIED FORWARD											
		YEAR-TO-DATE TOTAL											

DECEMBER EXPENSE REPORT

DATE	PAYMENT TYPE cash, check #, cc #, debit	PURCHASED FROM	PURCHASE TOTAL	TAXES & LICENSES	TRAVEL & ENTERTAINMENT	FOOD	TOYS	HOUSEHOLD ITEMS	CLEANING SUPPLIES	ACTIVITY EXPENSES			MILES
		THIS MONTH'S TOTAL											
		BALANCE CARRIED FORWARD											
		YEAR-TO-DATE TOTAL											

See page 85 for an explanation of how to transfer expenses to your tax forms. You may wish to relabel the columns to fit your business needs.

See page 6 for an explanation of the order in which we present the categories.

HOUSE EXPENSES WORKSHEET

YEAR:	Natural Gas		Electricity		Water/Sewer		Trash Collection		Cable TV	
	Date Paid	Amount	Date Paid	Amount	Date Paid	Amount	Date Paid	Amount	Date Paid	Amount
JANUARY										
FEBRUARY										
MARCH										
APRIL										
MAY										
JUNE										
JULY										
AUGUST										
SEPTEMBER										
OCTOBER										
NOVEMBER										
DECEMBER										
TOTAL										
TIME-SPACE PERCENTAGE										
FCC BUSINESS EXPENSE										

Homeowners Insurance		Property Taxes		Mortgage Interest or Rent		House Repairs & Maintenance	
Date Paid	Amount	Date Paid	Amount	Date Paid	Amount	Date Paid	Amount

NOTE: You are entitled to claim a portion of these house expenses for your business. Use this worksheet to record these expenses each month or once a year. For each column, fill in the total and your Time-Space percentage (to compute, see the *Family Child Care Record-Keeping Guide*, 9th edition). To arrive at the FCC business expense, multiply the total in each column by the Time-Space percentage.

Add together the FCC business expenses for natural gas, electricity, water/sewer, trash collection, and cable TV, and enter the total under Utilities on the next page. Take the totals of the other FCC business expense columns and enter them on the next page. When you file your taxes, the house expenses on this page go directly onto Form 8829 Expenses for Business Use of Your Home.

INCOME TAX WORKSHEET

TOTAL INCOME (See December Year-to-Date Total. Enter directly onto Form 1040 Schedule C.)	
EXPENSES	
I. DIRECT BUSINESS EXPENSES (See monthly expense reports. Enter directly onto Form 1040 Schedule C.)	
ADVERTISING	
CAR AND TRUCK EXPENSES (Include mileage and the business portion of any car-loan interest or excise tax.)	
LIABILITY INSURANCE	
BUSINESS INTEREST (not mortgage interest) (credit card interest on business portion of purchases)	
LEGAL AND PROFESSIONAL SERVICES	
OFFICE EXPENSES (postage, bank charges, education and training, dues, publications)	
RENT OF BUSINESS PROPERTY (other than home or apartment) (videos, carpet shampooer)	
REPAIRS AND MAINTENANCE OF PERSONAL PROPERTY (furniture, appliances, equipment)	
SUPPLIES	
TAXES AND LICENSES	
TRAVEL AND ENTERTAINMENT (for overnight conferences)	
FOOD (List under Other Expenses on Form 1040 Schedule C.)	
TOYS (List under Other Expenses on Form 1040 Schedule C.)	
HOUSEHOLD ITEMS, CLEANING SUPPLIES, AND ACTIVITY EXPENSES (List under Other Expenses on Form 1040 Schedule C.)	
II. HOUSE EXPENSES (See page 84. Enter directly onto Form 8829.)	
UTILITIES	
HOMEOWNERS INSURANCE	
PROPERTY TAXES	
MORTGAGE INTEREST OR RENT	
HOUSE REPAIRS AND MAINTENANCE (painting, broken glass)	
III. DEPRECIATION EXPENSES (Enter directly onto Form 8829 or Form 4562.)	
HOUSE (Form 8829)	
HOME IMPROVEMENTS (Form 4562) (new roof, furnace, remodeling)	
LAND IMPROVEMENTS (Form 4562 or Schedule C) (fence, driveway)	
TOTAL EXPENSES (deductions)	
NET INCOME (income minus expenses)	

How to Use This Worksheet

Use this worksheet at the end of the year to pull together all of your business expenses recorded on this *Redleaf Calendar-Keeper*. The categories of expenses listed here correspond to particular lines on the various tax forms that you must fill out for your business. Enter direct business expenses on Form 1040 Schedule C. Enter house expenses on Form 8829. Enter depreciation expenses on Form 8829 or Form 4562. After you have completed Forms 8829 and 4562, you will enter the totals from these forms onto your Schedule C.

You may wish to add or move some direct business expenses to different categories than are shown on this worksheet. Sometimes you may have two or more different expense categories on one receipt. You may either split the receipt and list items under more than one category or list all the expenses under one category. It doesn't matter which method you choose because all direct business expenses get totaled at the bottom of the Schedule C. You will not be penalized by the IRS for listing a supply expense under the food category or vice versa.

There are special rules concerning depreciation expenses. For a description of how to calculate depreciation expenses, see the *Family Child Care 2025 Tax Workbook and Organizer*.

PAYMENT AND INCOME RECORD FOR JANUARY–MARCH

CHILD'S NAME	JANUARY						JAN TOTAL	FEBRUARY						FEB TOTAL	MARCH						MAR TOTAL	1st Qtr* Total
SUBTOTALS																						
FOOD PROGRAM																						
OTHER INCOME																						
TOTALS																						

*1st quarter for estimated tax for the months of January–March. For income tax purposes, quarters are determined by the federal government and are not always the same as calendar quarters. Taxes for the 1st quarter are due April 15.

If you receive payments from a third party (such as a government agency) and don't get paid until a later month, use two lines per child and enter the payment date and check number on the second line.

PAYMENT AND INCOME RECORD FOR JANUARY–MARCH CONTINUED

CHILD'S NAME	JANUARY						JAN TOTAL	FEBRUARY						FEB TOTAL	MARCH						MAR TOTAL	1st Qtr* Total
SUBTOTALS																						
FOOD PROGRAM																						
OTHER INCOME																						
TOTALS																						

*1st quarter for estimated tax for the months of January–March. For income tax purposes, quarters are determined by the federal government and are not always the same as calendar quarters. Taxes for the 1st quarter are due April 15.

PAYMENT AND INCOME RECORD FOR APRIL–JUNE

CHILD'S NAME	APRIL						APR TOTAL	MAY						MAY TOTAL	2nd Qtr* TOTAL	JUNE						JUN TOTAL
SUBTOTALS																						
FOOD PROGRAM																						
OTHER INCOME																						
TOTALS																						

*2nd quarter for estimated tax for the months of April and May. For income tax purposes, quarters are determined by the federal government and are not always the same as calendar quarters. Taxes for the 2nd quarter are due June 16.

BALANCE CARRIED FORWARD

YEAR-TO-DATE TOTAL

PAYMENT AND INCOME RECORD FOR APRIL–JUNE CONTINUED

CHILD'S NAME	APRIL							APR TOTAL	MAY							MAY TOTAL	2nd Qtr* TOTAL	JUNE							JUN TOTAL
SUBTOTALS																									
FOOD PROGRAM																									
OTHER INCOME																									
TOTALS																									

BALANCE CARRIED FORWARD

YEAR-TO-DATE TOTAL

*2nd quarter for estimated tax for the months of April and May. For income tax purposes, quarters are determined by the federal government and are not always the same as calendar quarters. Taxes for the 2nd quarter are due June 16.

PAYMENT AND INCOME RECORD FOR JULY–SEPTEMBER

CHILD'S NAME	JULY						JUL TOTAL	AUGUST						AUG TOTAL	3rd Qtr* TOTAL	SEPTEMBER						SEP TOTAL
SUBTOTALS																						
FOOD PROGRAM																						
OTHER INCOME																						
TOTALS																						

*3rd quarter for estimated tax for the months of June–August. For income tax purposes, quarters are determined by the federal government and are not always the same as calendar quarters. Taxes for the 3rd quarter are due September 15.

BALANCE CARRIED FORWARD

YEAR-TO-DATE TOTAL

PAYMENT AND INCOME RECORD FOR JULY–SEPTEMBER CONTINUED

CHILD'S NAME	JULY					JUL TOTAL	AUGUST					AUG TOTAL	3rd Qtr* TOTAL	SEPTEMBER					SEP TOTAL
SUBTOTALS																			
FOOD PROGRAM																			
OTHER INCOME																			
TOTALS																			

*3rd quarter for estimated tax for the months of June–August. For income tax purposes, quarters are determined by the federal government and are not always the same as calendar quarters. Taxes for the 3rd quarter are due September 15.

BALANCE CARRIED FORWARD

YEAR-TO-DATE TOTAL

PAYMENT AND INCOME RECORD FOR OCTOBER–DECEMBER

CHILD'S NAME	OCTOBER						OCT TOTAL	NOVEMBER						NOV TOTAL	DECEMBER						DEC TOTAL	4th Qtr* TOTAL
SUBTOTALS																						
FOOD PROGRAM																						
OTHER INCOME																						
TOTALS																						

*4th quarter for estimated tax for the months of September–December. For income tax purposes, quarters are determined by the federal government and are not always the same as calendar quarters. Taxes for the 4th quarter are due January 15, 2026.

Income should be reported as income in the year you receive it, not the year you earn it. Payments received after December 31, 2024, for child care services you delivered in 2024 should be reported as income in 2025.

BALANCE CARRIED FORWARD

2025 TOTAL

PAYMENT AND INCOME RECORD FOR OCTOBER–DECEMBER CONTINUED

CHILD'S NAME	OCTOBER						OCT TOTAL	NOVEMBER						NOV TOTAL	DECEMBER						DEC TOTAL	4th Qtr* TOTAL
SUBTOTALS																						
FOOD PROGRAM																						
OTHER INCOME																						
TOTALS																						

*4th quarter for estimated tax for the months of September–December. For income tax purposes, quarters are determined by the federal government and are not always the same as calendar quarters. Taxes for the 4th quarter are due January 15, 2026.

Income should be reported as income in the year you receive it, not the year you earn it. Payments received after December 31, 2024, for child care services you delivered in 2024 should be reported as income in 2025.

BALANCE CARRIED FORWARD

2025 TOTAL

MEAL FORM Week of _____ 2025

Child	Mon	Tue	Wed	Thu	Fri	Sat	Sun	Totals	Child	Mon	Tue	Wed	Thu	Fri	Sat	Sun	Totals
	Bkst ___ Lun ___ Din ___ Sn1 ___ Sn2 ___ Sn3 ___	Bkst ___ Lun ___ Din ___ Sn1 ___ Sn2 ___ Sn3 ___	Bkst ___ Lun ___ Din ___ Sn1 ___ Sn2 ___ Sn3 ___	Bkst ___ Lun ___ Din ___ Sn1 ___ Sn2 ___ Sn3 ___	Bkst ___ Lun ___ Din ___ Sn1 ___ Sn2 ___ Sn3 ___	Bkst ___ Lun ___ Din ___ Sn1 ___ Sn2 ___ Sn3 ___	Bkst ___ Lun ___ Din ___ Sn1 ___ Sn2 ___ Sn3 ___	B ___ L ___ D ___ S ___		Bkst ___ Lun ___ Din ___ Sn1 ___ Sn2 ___ Sn3 ___	Bkst ___ Lun ___ Din ___ Sn1 ___ Sn2 ___ Sn3 ___	Bkst ___ Lun ___ Din ___ Sn1 ___ Sn2 ___ Sn3 ___	Bkst ___ Lun ___ Din ___ Sn1 ___ Sn2 ___ Sn3 ___	Bkst ___ Lun ___ Din ___ Sn1 ___ Sn2 ___ Sn3 ___	Bkst ___ Lun ___ Din ___ Sn1 ___ Sn2 ___ Sn3 ___	Bkst ___ Lun ___ Din ___ Sn1 ___ Sn2 ___ Sn3 ___	B ___ L ___ D ___ S ___
	Bkst ___ Lun ___ Din ___ Sn1 ___ Sn2 ___ Sn3 ___	Bkst ___ Lun ___ Din ___ Sn1 ___ Sn2 ___ Sn3 ___	Bkst ___ Lun ___ Din ___ Sn1 ___ Sn2 ___ Sn3 ___	Bkst ___ Lun ___ Din ___ Sn1 ___ Sn2 ___ Sn3 ___	Bkst ___ Lun ___ Din ___ Sn1 ___ Sn2 ___ Sn3 ___	Bkst ___ Lun ___ Din ___ Sn1 ___ Sn2 ___ Sn3 ___	Bkst ___ Lun ___ Din ___ Sn1 ___ Sn2 ___ Sn3 ___	B ___ L ___ D ___ S ___		Bkst ___ Lun ___ Din ___ Sn1 ___ Sn2 ___ Sn3 ___	Bkst ___ Lun ___ Din ___ Sn1 ___ Sn2 ___ Sn3 ___	Bkst ___ Lun ___ Din ___ Sn1 ___ Sn2 ___ Sn3 ___	Bkst ___ Lun ___ Din ___ Sn1 ___ Sn2 ___ Sn3 ___	Bkst ___ Lun ___ Din ___ Sn1 ___ Sn2 ___ Sn3 ___	Bkst ___ Lun ___ Din ___ Sn1 ___ Sn2 ___ Sn3 ___	Bkst ___ Lun ___ Din ___ Sn1 ___ Sn2 ___ Sn3 ___	B ___ L ___ D ___ S ___
	Bkst ___ Lun ___ Din ___ Sn1 ___ Sn2 ___ Sn3 ___	Bkst ___ Lun ___ Din ___ Sn1 ___ Sn2 ___ Sn3 ___	Bkst ___ Lun ___ Din ___ Sn1 ___ Sn2 ___ Sn3 ___	Bkst ___ Lun ___ Din ___ Sn1 ___ Sn2 ___ Sn3 ___	Bkst ___ Lun ___ Din ___ Sn1 ___ Sn2 ___ Sn3 ___	Bkst ___ Lun ___ Din ___ Sn1 ___ Sn2 ___ Sn3 ___	Bkst ___ Lun ___ Din ___ Sn1 ___ Sn2 ___ Sn3 ___	B ___ L ___ D ___ S ___		Bkst ___ Lun ___ Din ___ Sn1 ___ Sn2 ___ Sn3 ___	Bkst ___ Lun ___ Din ___ Sn1 ___ Sn2 ___ Sn3 ___	Bkst ___ Lun ___ Din ___ Sn1 ___ Sn2 ___ Sn3 ___	Bkst ___ Lun ___ Din ___ Sn1 ___ Sn2 ___ Sn3 ___	Bkst ___ Lun ___ Din ___ Sn1 ___ Sn2 ___ Sn3 ___	Bkst ___ Lun ___ Din ___ Sn1 ___ Sn2 ___ Sn3 ___	Bkst ___ Lun ___ Din ___ Sn1 ___ Sn2 ___ Sn3 ___	B ___ L ___ D ___ S ___
	Bkst ___ Lun ___ Din ___ Sn1 ___ Sn2 ___ Sn3 ___	Bkst ___ Lun ___ Din ___ Sn1 ___ Sn2 ___ Sn3 ___	Bkst ___ Lun ___ Din ___ Sn1 ___ Sn2 ___ Sn3 ___	Bkst ___ Lun ___ Din ___ Sn1 ___ Sn2 ___ Sn3 ___	Bkst ___ Lun ___ Din ___ Sn1 ___ Sn2 ___ Sn3 ___	Bkst ___ Lun ___ Din ___ Sn1 ___ Sn2 ___ Sn3 ___	Bkst ___ Lun ___ Din ___ Sn1 ___ Sn2 ___ Sn3 ___	B ___ L ___ D ___ S ___		Bkst ___ Lun ___ Din ___ Sn1 ___ Sn2 ___ Sn3 ___	Bkst ___ Lun ___ Din ___ Sn1 ___ Sn2 ___ Sn3 ___	Bkst ___ Lun ___ Din ___ Sn1 ___ Sn2 ___ Sn3 ___	Bkst ___ Lun ___ Din ___ Sn1 ___ Sn2 ___ Sn3 ___	Bkst ___ Lun ___ Din ___ Sn1 ___ Sn2 ___ Sn3 ___	Bkst ___ Lun ___ Din ___ Sn1 ___ Sn2 ___ Sn3 ___	Bkst ___ Lun ___ Din ___ Sn1 ___ Sn2 ___ Sn3 ___	B ___ L ___ D ___ S ___
	Bkst ___ Lun ___ Din ___ Sn1 ___ Sn2 ___ Sn3 ___	Bkst ___ Lun ___ Din ___ Sn1 ___ Sn2 ___ Sn3 ___	Bkst ___ Lun ___ Din ___ Sn1 ___ Sn2 ___ Sn3 ___	Bkst ___ Lun ___ Din ___ Sn1 ___ Sn2 ___ Sn3 ___	Bkst ___ Lun ___ Din ___ Sn1 ___ Sn2 ___ Sn3 ___	Bkst ___ Lun ___ Din ___ Sn1 ___ Sn2 ___ Sn3 ___	Bkst ___ Lun ___ Din ___ Sn1 ___ Sn2 ___ Sn3 ___	B ___ L ___ D ___ S ___		Bkst ___ Lun ___ Din ___ Sn1 ___ Sn2 ___ Sn3 ___	Bkst ___ Lun ___ Din ___ Sn1 ___ Sn2 ___ Sn3 ___	Bkst ___ Lun ___ Din ___ Sn1 ___ Sn2 ___ Sn3 ___	Bkst ___ Lun ___ Din ___ Sn1 ___ Sn2 ___ Sn3 ___	Bkst ___ Lun ___ Din ___ Sn1 ___ Sn2 ___ Sn3 ___	Bkst ___ Lun ___ Din ___ Sn1 ___ Sn2 ___ Sn3 ___	Bkst ___ Lun ___ Din ___ Sn1 ___ Sn2 ___ Sn3 ___	B ___ L ___ D ___ S ___
	Bkst ___ Lun ___ Din ___ Sn1 ___ Sn2 ___ Sn3 ___	Bkst ___ Lun ___ Din ___ Sn1 ___ Sn2 ___ Sn3 ___	Bkst ___ Lun ___ Din ___ Sn1 ___ Sn2 ___ Sn3 ___	Bkst ___ Lun ___ Din ___ Sn1 ___ Sn2 ___ Sn3 ___	Bkst ___ Lun ___ Din ___ Sn1 ___ Sn2 ___ Sn3 ___	Bkst ___ Lun ___ Din ___ Sn1 ___ Sn2 ___ Sn3 ___	Bkst ___ Lun ___ Din ___ Sn1 ___ Sn2 ___ Sn3 ___	B ___ L ___ D ___ S ___		Bkst ___ Lun ___ Din ___ Sn1 ___ Sn2 ___ Sn3 ___	Bkst ___ Lun ___ Din ___ Sn1 ___ Sn2 ___ Sn3 ___	Bkst ___ Lun ___ Din ___ Sn1 ___ Sn2 ___ Sn3 ___	Bkst ___ Lun ___ Din ___ Sn1 ___ Sn2 ___ Sn3 ___	Bkst ___ Lun ___ Din ___ Sn1 ___ Sn2 ___ Sn3 ___	Bkst ___ Lun ___ Din ___ Sn1 ___ Sn2 ___ Sn3 ___	Bkst ___ Lun ___ Din ___ Sn1 ___ Sn2 ___ Sn3 ___	B ___ L ___ D ___ S ___

Place a check mark (✓) next to each meal or snack you serve. Do not count meals served to your own children. If you are on the Food Program, use this form to track your nonreimbursed meals only. Add the reimbursed meals from your monthly claim forms and the nonreimbursed meals from this form together, and put the totals on the year-end meal tally on page 95. If you are not on the Food Program, use this form to track all your meals, and put the totals on the year-end meal tally on page 95.

Make copies of this form for each week of the year. If you have six or fewer children in your program, you can use one form for two weeks. You can download this form at the Redleaf Press website. Go to www.redleafpress.org, and find the page for the *Redleaf Calendar-Keeper 2025*. There will be a link to this form.

Weekly Totals

Breakfasts _____   Dinners _____

Lunches _____   Snacks _____

YEAR-END MEAL TALLY

If you are not on the Food Program, enter all meals and snacks in the column labeled "Number Not Reimbursed by Food Program."

	Breakfasts		Lunches		Dinners		Snacks	
	Number Reimbursed by Food Program	Number Not Reimbursed by Food Program	Number Reimbursed by Food Program	Number Not Reimbursed by Food Program	Number Reimbursed by Food Program	Number Not Reimbursed by Food Program	Number Reimbursed by Food Program	Number Not Reimbursed by Food Program
January								
February								
March								
April								
May								
June								
July								
August								
September								
October								
November								
December								
TOTAL								

2025 Standard Meal Allowance Rate*

Number of Breakfasts	_____	X	$1.66	=	$_____
Number of Lunches	_____	X	$3.15	=	$_____
Number of Dinners	_____	X	$3.15	=	$_____
Number of Snacks	_____	X	$0.93	=	$_____
			Total Food Deductions		$_____ †

Do not report any meals served to your own children (even if they are reimbursed by the Food Program).

* The IRS standard meal allowance rate for 2025 used in these calculations is based on the Tier I rate as of January 1, 2025. This rate is used for all meals and snacks served throughout 2025, even though the Tier I rate goes up every July. All providers, whether on Tier I or Tier II (and all providers not on the Food Program), will use the rates listed.

† Enter this amount on Form 1040 Schedule C, Part V. Be sure to enter any reimbursements from the Food Program (with the exception of reimbursements for your own children) as income on Form 1040 Schedule C, line 6.

EMERGENCY PHONE NUMBERS

PROVIDER'S ADDRESS		FIRE		POLICE		**IN EMERGENCIES**
		EMERGENCY SQUAD		POISON CONTROL CENTER		**USE 911**
PROVIDER'S PHONE #		LOCAL HOSPITAL		OTHER		**IF AVAILABLE**

Child's Name	Birth Date	Parent / Guardian		Parent / Guardian		Emergency Contact		Doctor	
		Name / Home #	Work # / Cell #	Name / Home #	Work # / Cell #	Name	Phone #	Name	Phone #

EMERGENCY PHONE NUMBERS (continued from page 96)

Child's Name	Birth Date	Parent / Guardian		Parent / Guardian		Emergency Contact		Doctor	
		Name / Home #	Work # / Cell #	Name / Home #	Work # / Cell #	Name	Phone #	Name	Phone #

WAITING LIST

Child's Name	Age	Parent/Guardian Names	Phone #	Date of Call	Date Needed
			W H W H		
			W H W H		
			W H W H		
			W H W H		
			W H W H		
			W H W H		
			W H W H		
			W H W H		
			W H W H		

EMERGENCY DRILL RECORD

	Time/Date	No. and Ages of Children	Type of Drill	Evac. Time
JAN			Fire	
FEB			Fire	
MAR			Fire	
APR			Fire	
MAY			Fire	
JUN			Fire	
JUL			Fire	
AUG			Fire	
SEP			Fire	
OCT			Fire	
NOV			Fire	
DEC			Fire	